new directions FOR INSTITUTIONAL RESEARCH

number 3
autumn 1974

new directions for institutional research

a quarterly sourcebook edited by Sidney Suslow and Paul Jedamus
and sponsored by the Association for Institutional Research

---

number 3
autumn 1974

toward affirmative action

lucy w. sells
issue editor

Jossey-Bass Inc., Publishers
San Francisco · Washington · London

TOWARD AFFIRMATIVE ACTION
New Directions for Institutional Research
Volume I, Number 3, Autumn 1974
Lucy W. Sells, Issue Editor

New Directions for Institutional Research is published quarterly by Jossey-Bass, Inc., Publishers, and is sponsored by the Association for Institutional Research. Subscriptions are available at the regular rate for institutions, libraries, and agencies of $25 for one year. Individuals may subscribe at the special professional rate of $15 for one year. *New Directions* is numbered sequentially—please order extra copies by sequential number. The volume and issue numbers above are included for the convenience of libraries.

Correspondence:
Subscriptions, single-issue orders, change of address notices, undelivered copies, and other correspondence should be sent to *New Directions* Subscriptions, Jossey-Bass, Inc., Publishers, 615 Montgomery Street, San Francisco, California 94111. Editorial correspondence should be sent to the Editor-in-Chief, Sidney Suslow, Institutional Research, 47 Campbell Hall, University of California, Berkeley, California 94720.

Library of Congress Catalogue Card Number LC 74-2341

Cover design by Willi Baum
Manufactured in the United States of America

contents

on institutional research and affirmative action *sidney suslow* ix

editor's notes: old directions of affirmative action *lucy w. sells* xi

the hand that rocked the cradle has learned to rock the boat *bernice sandler* 1

An introduction to affirmative action for women in higher education, from the point of view of a leading advocate.

on discrimination: part one *sidney hook* 23

The dangers of present federal policies on affirmative action, as seen by a leading adversary.

on discrimination: part two *miro m. todorovich* 31

Alternatives to present policies, from a second opponent: coordinator of the Committee on Academic Nondiscrimination and Integrity.

affirmative action: myth and reality *peter e. holmes* 39

The perspective of an enforcer: the director of the Office for Civil Rights in the Department of Health, Education, and Welfare.

implications for institutions *robert l. johnson* 55

How the University of California is approaching affirmative action may have implications for decision-makers and planners elsewhere.

implications for government *robben w. fleming* 65

Reasons for needed changes in federal policy, based on the arbitration experience of the president of the University of Michigan.

critical points for affirmative action *lucy w. sells* 71

Five major decision points affect the availability of women and minorities for professorships.

new directions for affirmative action *lucy w. sells* 87

Recommendations for next steps together with advice about additional resources on the problem of equal rights in higher education.

index 97

The Association for Institutional Research was created in 1966 to benefit, assist, and advance research leading to improved understanding, planning, and operation of institutions of higher education. Publication policy is set by its Publications Board.

on institutional research and affirmative action

If you are an institutional researcher or academic planner, whether you are an advocate or an adversary of the aims of affirmative action in our colleges and universities you cannot avoid involvement with these aims. A paucity of information deprives both advocates and adversaries of opportunities to present evidence in support of their positions and deprives campus administrators of the facts needed for policy formulation and for day-to-day decisions.

What are the real availability pools of women and ethnic minorities at your institution for student admissions, faculty positions, and staff openings? What are the distributions of assessable characteristics among applicants which meet, exceed, or fall below your institution's criteria for admissions and employment? What instruments need to be constructed or employed to measure trends in improved entry of women and minorities to curricula and jobs and in promotions and salary increments?

Professional researchers and planners must address themselves to these and numerous other questions on issues of equal rights if institutions are to implement equitable policies and decisions. Additionally, the current extraordinary costs of gathering, compiling, and analyzing data for affirmative actions programs, as noted in this issue, should stimulate institutional researchers to seek new methods, new systems, and perhaps even new definitions which will substantially reduce these costs. Because institutional researchers have a role to evaluate available information on affirmative action and to recommend changes where necessary in institutional data gathering and institutional policies, we devote this issue of *New Directions for Institutional Research* to a wide-ranging synthesis of views on affirmative action and its implications for colleges and universities.

Sidney Suslow
Editor-in-Chief

editor's notes: old directions of affirmative action

Institutions of higher education are caught in the conflict between federal policy on affirmative action for equal rights with respect to women and minorities, and their need to retain autonomy with respect to standards of scholarship and excellence in the recruitment, hiring, and promotion of faculty members. In working on affirmative action with students, faculty members, administrators, legislators, and federal compliance officials, I have observed three very different subcultures. They consist of people with such different perspectives on the myths and realities of affirmative action that they tend to talk past each other from their respective viewpoints instead of dealing directly with each other.

These subcultures can be characterized as the *advocates, adversaries,* and *enforcers* of affirmative action. The primary source of paralysis in achieving affirmative action, which is just now beginning to be resolved, has been the conflict among these three groups. Discussion between and among them has taken place in a context of mistrust, ill will, and closed communication. The hostility and suspicion between and among them has been generated by differing interpretations of the data on sex and ethnic differences in educational achievement, by differing perceptions of the goals and consequences of affirmative action, and by differing perceptions of the three respective commitments and motivations to achieve affirmative action.

the advocates

Advocates of affirmative action attribute the different distribution of women and minorities, compared to white males, to a systematic exclusionary process on the part of institutions of higher education. They perceive affirmative action as necessary to achieve high standards of scholarship and excellence, and they are convinced that merit, rather than sex or ethnicity, should be the sole criterion for recruitment, hiring, and promotion. They are trying to develop merit evaluations which do not start with the idea that being female, or belonging to an ethnic minority is, by definition, an imperfection.

Bernice Sandler is a leading representative of the advocate's most constructive perspective. In the first chapter of this issue she reviews the legislation regarding discrimination in higher education, summarizes the problems faced by colleges and universities, and analyzes some of the myths of affirmative action as seen by its advocates. There is a less constructive wing of the advocate's perspective. Those who have not yet tasted the rewards of success in the academic system are especially hostile and suspicious of the adversaries of affirmative action, whom they see as deliberately trying to exclude them from the system. Some suspect the enforcers of not trying hard enough to include them into the system. Some even see the adversaries and enforcers in deliberate collusion to bar them from success.

the adversaries

Adversaries of affirmative action tend to interpret the differential distribution of women and minorities in the academic system not as a problem of the system but rather as the result of differing levels of talent, energy, ambitions, and aspirations on the part of women and minorities. They feel coerced and constrained both by the external pressure from the enforcers and by the internal demands of the advocates of affirmative action. In particular, they are convinced that the values of scholarship and excellence will be destroyed by affirmative action, most often because they misinterpret affirmative action to mean that whenever a woman or minority person competes with a white man for a job, preference must be given to the woman or minority person even if the white man is better qualified. (In fact, as Sandler points out, federal policy states that only "when there has been a history or pattern of exclusion and/or discrimination, *and* if two candidates are equally qualified" can preference be given to the member of the excluded group.)

Sidney Hook and Miro Todorovich represent the most constructive wing of the adversaries' position. The less constructive wing rests on two assumptions which are untenable to the advocates and enforcers of affirmative action. The first is that there are no qualified women and minorities in the availability pools for faculty recruitment, hiring, and promotion. This assumption is insulting both to the highly qualified people who have earned their doctorates and are already part of the availability pool, and to those who might become part of the availability pool if given an opportunity to do so. The second is that faculty members, department chairmen, deans, and chancellors are such spineless creatures that they will sell out standards of scholarship and excellence by hiring unqualified women and minorities, rather than risk loss of federal funds by failure to meet goals. This is insulting to administrators of good will at every level who are making good faith efforts in recruitment.

the enforcers

Compliance enforcers at the state and federal levels perceive the goals of affirmative action as freeing all persons, independently of sex or ethnicity, to rise to the limits of their talents and energies. Like the advocates, they attribute the differential distribution of women and minorities to the exclusionary practices of the academic system and they view affirmative action as strengthening standards of scholarship and excellence, while the adversaries are equally convinced that it will destroy them. The enforcers feel constrained by conflicting accusations of the advocates and adversaries: first, that they are not doing enough for women and minorities, and second, that they are doing too much, to the detriment of white men.

Peter E. Holmes, director of the Office of Civil Rights of the Department of Health, Education, and Welfare, represents the most constructive of the enforcers' perspectives. A less constructive segment of enforcers is convinced that the adversaries of affirmative action have been recalcitrant because of their deliberate, conscious sexism and racism. Their paternalistic authoritarianism, which assumes the worst about institutions of higher education, and about the adversaries within those institutions, is as fundamental to the paralysis of affirmative action as is the sexism and racism of which they accuse the adversaries.

Most recently, at hearings on the civil rights obligations of institutions of higher education called by the Special Subcommittee on Education of the Committee on Education and Labor of the House of Representatives, where the authors represented in this issue of *New Directions for Institutional Research* testified, I observed that each of the three groups tends to think of itself as hero or victim, and those above in the hierarchy of power and authority as the villain, regardless of position on the ladder—whether within institutions of higher education, or between institutions and the Department of Health, Education, and Welfare. The major themes emerging from my own research on sex and ethnic differences in educational achievement are the automatic and unconscious assumptions about human beings, based on their own sex, ethnicity, and status, that have come to be labeled *sexism, racism,* and *authoritarianism.* These assumptions are so pervasive in the structure of society and personality that they are as invisible to those of us constrained by them as the air we breathe. *Authoritarianism* involves a profound sense of mistrust of people at different levels of power from one's own. It consists of an implicit assumption that persons at higher levels of power will behave like bad parents—either as bad fathers, who will punish them, or as bad mothers, who will neglect them—and that persons at lower levels of power will behave as bad children—either as bad sons, for compulsive rebellion, or as bad daughters, for compulsive docility.

This phenomenon of authoritarianism can be observed as a fundamental pathology of most hiearchical relations as well: between students and faculty members; faculty members and administrators; campus administrators and university-wide administrators; university-wide administrators and the legislature or governor; institutions of higher education and the Department of Health, Education, and Welfare; and HEW and members of Congress. Like sexism and racism, authoritarianism is internalized as need dispositions in individual personalities and is institutionalized as role expectations about human behavior. Paralysis and lack of productivity in affirmative action within institutions of higher education or between them and the Department of Health, Education, and Welfare, come not only from conflict among the three groups about the goals to achieve, the means of achieving them, and the standards of evaluation of achievement, but also by these implicit assumptions about individuals and groups.

The first step in the process of accommodation is to clarify the nature and extent of the conflict, by articulating and identifying the goals to be achieved, the means of achieving them, and the standards of evaluation of achievement. To this end, two articles in this volume, by Robert L. Johnson, vice president for university relations of the University of California, and Robben W. Fleming, president of the University of Michigan—two universities recently caught in the conflict over affirmative action—recommend steps that institutions and the federal government can take in this direction. I end this volume with some suggestions for achieving equal rights in higher education while at the same time retaining existing academic standards.

The realities of affirmative action are less dangerous for institutions of higher education than the myths the adversaries believe. It is hoped that this issue of *New Directions for Institutional Research* will provide a context for synthesizing the best of the perspectives of advocates, adversaries, and enforcers of affirmative action, in order to free all persons to rise to the limits of their talents and energies, independently of sex or ethnicity.

Lucy W. Sells
Issue Editor

A leading advocate of affirmative action reviews the legislation regarding discrimination in higher education, summarizes the issues faced by colleges and universities, and analyzes some of the myths of affirmative action as seen by its advocates.

the hand that rocked the cradle has learned to rock the boat

bernice sandler

Until very recently, sex discrimination on the campus, whether against faculty, staff, or students, was largely unnoticed, unchallenged, and unchecked. Indeed, such discrimination against most women in the academic community was legal: only an executive order forbidding discrimination in employment by federal contractors applied, and educational institutions without federal contracts could legally discriminate against women faculty and students. Prior to 1970, however, the executive order was not enforced with regard to sex or racial discrimination in universities.

The 92nd Congress, in a little noticed legislative explosion, articulated a national policy to end sex discrimination on the campus. Title VII of the Civil Rights Act of 1964, which forbids discrimination in employment, was extended to cover all educational institutions whether or not they receive federal monies; the Equal

Pay Act was extended to cover all administrative, executive, and professional employees, so that faculty are now covered; and Title IX of the Education Amendments Act of 1972 was enacted to forbid sex discrimination against students and employees in federally assisted education programs. There was virtually no opposition to the passage of these laws by either the educational community or the public at large. Discrimination, once only a philosophical or moral issue, is now a legal issue as well.

affirmative action legislation

Four separate sets of federal regulations and laws now cover discrimination in institutions of higher education.

Executive Order 11246 as Amended by Executive Order 11375. The executive order covers only those institutions which hold federal contracts. It prohibits discrimination in employment. It is not law, but a series of rules and regulations which contractors agree to follow when they accept a federal contract. Its main provision is that the contractor must have a written plan of affirmative action to "remedy the effects of past discrimination" and to prevent the continuation of current discrimination. The Department of Labor through its Office of Federal Contract Compliance is responsible for all policy matters under the executive order; the Department of Health, Education, and Welfare, however, does the actual review and enforcement in universities and colleges.

Institutions which voluntarily agree to provide a service to the government by way of a contract are required to undertake affirmative action regardless of whether or not there has been a finding of discrimination. Such action includes, but is not limited to, numerical goals. (In contrast, monies having the purpose of assisting the institution—rather than providing a service to the government—carry no affirmative action requirement.) Should an institution fail to follow the requirements of the executive order, contracts can be delayed, suspended, or terminated.

The Equal Pay Act of 1963 as Amended by Title IX of the Education Amendments of 1972. In the Educational Amendments Act of 1972 there is a little-noted section that extends the coverage of the Equal Pay Act of 1963 to executive, administrative, and professional employees, including all faculty. It is enforced by the Wage and Hour Division of the Employment Standards Administration of the Department of Labor. Like the Executive Order, but unlike Title VII, reviews can be conducted without prior complaint. The Equal Pay Act was the first sex discrimination legislation enacted and has been successful in getting nonprofessional women millions of dollars in back pay.

After a review is conducted, if a violation is found, the employer is asked to settle on the spot, namely, to raise the wages and pay back pay to the underpaid workers. Should the employer refuse (and most don't, as 95 percent of the cases are settled without recourse to litigation), the Department of Labor is authorized to go to court. No affirmative action is required other than back pay.

Title IX of the Education Amendments of 1972 (Higher Education Act). Title IX forbids discrimination on the basis of sex in all federally assisted education programs. Both students and employees are covered. All institutions, whether public or private, that receive federal monies by way of a grant, loan, or contract are covered. Title IX is patterned after Title VI of the Civil Rights Act of 1964 which forbids discrimination on the basis of race, color, and national origin in all federally assisted programs. The Department of Health, Education, and Welfare (HEW) is the enforcement agency. Affirmative action is not required but can be imposed after a finding of discrimination.

Title VII of the Civil Rights Act of 1964 as Amended by the Equal Employment Opportunity Act of 1972. Title VII was amended on March 24, 1972, to cover educational institutions and forbids discrimination on the basis of race, color, national origin, religion, and sex in employment by unions and by employers. It applies to all institutions, public or private, whether or not they receive any federal funds. Title VII is enforced by the Equal Employment Opportunity Commission (EEOC), which is appointed by the president. However, unlike the executive order, no affirmative action is required; employers are required merely to note discrimination in employment. A conciliation agreement or court order may require affirmative action, but this would be after a finding of discrimination. Should conciliation fail, the EEOC can take an employer to court.

The basic body of legal principles applying to employment discrimination have been developed in Title VII litigation and in cases involving the Fifth and Fourteenth Amendments of the Constitution.

Academics have been puzzled and somewhat bewildered by the impact of these new laws. Many institutions holding federal contracts had already felt the sting of the federal government under Executive Order 11246 as amended, but the new legislation has raised new questions and concerns within the academic community as to how federal law impacts upon the traditional employment practices of academia.

when is affirmative action required?

Institutions of higher education can become involved with affirmative action in any of the following ways:
1. Any institution can voluntarily develop an affirmative action plan.
2. Institutions which voluntarily accept a government contract are required to develop affirmative action plans, including numerical goals.
3. An institution which has been charged with discrimination under Title VII, the Fourteenth Amendment, the Fifth Amendment, Title IX, and possibly the Civil Rights Acts of 1866 and 1871, may be required to develop affirmative action procedures as a result of conciliation or as a private settlement of a suit under these laws. Numerical goals may be included.
4. If conciliation or private settlement of a suit has failed, the court may impose affirmative action requirements, including numerical goals.

The following list of issues, compiled for the Association of American College's Project on the Status and Education of Women, are arising on many campuses. While by no means exhaustive, these twenty-five items are among the major ones faced by administrators under federal laws and regulations. Unless otherwise noted, both Executive Order 11246 and Title VII of the Civil Rights Act apply.

1. Affirmative Action Plans. Required of all institutions with federal contracts totaling $50,000 or more and having fifty or more employees. Revised Order No. 4 details what these plans must cover. Public institutions have previously been exempt from the requirement of having a *written* plan. As of January 19, 1972, this exemption was removed.

2. Numerical Goals and Timetables. Required of all institutions with federal contracts covered by the executive order. President Nixon reaffirmed (August 11, 1972) federal policy which forbids quotas but upholds goals. Such goals are based on the available pool of qualified persons and in line with anticipated vacancies and may be projected in terms of percentages or actual numbers.

The institution must document its "good faith" efforts. What did it do to recruit women and minorities? Were they interviewed? What was the decision? And so on. The obligation to meet the goal is not absolute; if the best qualified person is white and male, he can be hired. But the institution must be able to document that effort was made to recruit women and minorities, that such candidates were treated fairly, and that the white male was indeed "better qualified."

The institution sets the criteria, not HEW. The criteria must be applied equally to men and women, whites and blacks, and must not be in itself discriminatory. Criteria which gave preference to people who did their undergraduate work at Ivy League schools would be discriminatory in that women have been denied, until very recently, the opportunity to attend such institutions.

In very limited instances only can preference be given to women and minorities: When there has been a history or pattern of exclusion or discrimination (or both), and if two candidates are equally qualified, only then can preference be given to the member of the excluded group.

3. Salary Equalization. Women and minorities cannot be paid less because of their sex or race. Bona fide merit systems are allowed, provided they are not discriminatory on the basis of race or sex. Criteria for raises must be applied equally. Numerous institutions have set aside specific sums for "equity adjustments" in order to compensate for past inequities to women and minorities. The Equal Pay Act also applies.

4. Back Pay. Title VII allows up to two years (but not prior to date of coverage—for professional staff: March 24, 1972). The Equal Pay Act allows up to two years for nonwillful violation and three years for a willful violation (but not prior to date of coverage —for professional staff: July 1, 1972). The executive order—time limit not clear. HEW will seek back pay only for those individuals who were not covered by other laws allowing back pay at the time of violation.

5. Pensions. Pensions such as TIAA which pay women less on a monthly basis because of acturial differences: Under the executive order, employers make either equal contributions or provide equal benefits. Under the stricter Title VII guidelines (April 5, 1972), equal benefits must be provided, regardless of the contribution.

6. Nepotism. Under Title VII and the executive order practices which restrict the employment of spouses are largely prohibited. (A policy which officially applied to all spouses but in practice applied mainly to wives would be illegal.) Institutions cannot prohibit spouses from working in the same department when both are qualified. To avoid conflict of interest, institutions can prohibit spouses from participating in employment decisions about each other. Such decisions, for example, when one is in a supervisory relationship to the other, can be delegated to someone else or to a committee. (See No. 16, *Marital and Parental Status.*)

7. Maternity Leave. Both Title VII and the executive order apply. Childbearing leave: Institutions are advised to follow the stricter Title VII guidelines which apply to all institutions, regardless of whether or not they receive federal aid. Title VII guidelines require that the part of pregnancy and childbirth when a woman is physically unable to work be treated like all other temporary disabilities in terms of sick leave, health insurance, and job retention. Childrearing leave: Under HEW guidelines, if leave is available for other personal reasons, it should be available for child*rearing* (when a woman is able to work but chooses not to). Such childrearing leave must be available to both sexes.

8. Internal Grievance Procedures. HEW does not require this but recommends that there be written procedures whereby individuals who feel aggrieved because of sex or racial discrimination can ask for investigation and, if necessary, redress.

9. Child Care. Not required by any of the laws but recommended by HEW guidelines. Many women's groups are pressing for such centers to be available to the children of staff, faculty, and students.

10. Recruitment and Hiring. Under the executive order, if current recruiting practices (such as word-of-mouth recruiting) result in a "significantly lower representation" of women and minorities in the applicant pool than would be expected from their availability in the labor force, then new sources of recruiting must be developed. Title VII policy is expected to be the same. HEW requires that standards and criteria should be "reasonably explicit" and be accessible to employees and applicants.

11. Affirmative Advertising. All notices of job openings in advertisements, flyers, or letters should indicate that applications from women and minorities are being sought, such as: "Women and minorities, including minority women, are welcome to apply." Employers cannot state that only members of a particular sex or race will be considered.

12. Policy Statements. Under the executive order institutions are required to have in writing a policy of nondiscrimination in employment. The statement must appear in personnel manuals and be disseminated throughout the campus.

13. Conditions of Employment, Salaries, and Benefits. Federal regulations and laws require that there be no discrimination in all conditions of employment, including: recruitment, hiring, layoff, discharge and recall, and inservice training; opportunities for promotion; participation in training programs; wages and salaries; sick leave time and pay; vacation time and pay; overtime work and pay; medical, hospital, life and accident insurance; and optional and compulsory retirement.

14. Inbred Hiring. Policies that forbid departments from hiring their own students upon degree completion decrease the available pool of qualified female applicants and work a particular hardship on married women who may not be mobile. Such policies may be a violation of the executive order and Title VII and need to be reevaluated.

15. Search Committees. HEW recommends that all search committees wherever possible should include women and minorities.

16. Marital and Parental Status. (See No. 6, *Nepotism.*) Discrimination on the basis of marital status is specifically forbidden by Title VII when such criteria are applied to one sex only. Although not specifically mentioned, criteria concerning parental status would also be a violation if only applied to one sex.

17. Monitoring and Accountability. Under the executive order, affirmative action plans are required to have a system of accountability and monitoring. 1) An institution-wide office must maintain records and monitor individual departments and units and report annually. 2) Individual departments and units are required to maintain records of all applicants and hires, as well as records of the efforts made to recruit women. Such records should allow for an ongoing analysis of all employment decisions: recruiting, hiring, promotions, and salary increases.

18. Job Analysis. Under the executive order, all job classifications must be reviewed in order to identify "underutilization" of women and minorities. Data should be provided simultaneously on race and sex (for instance black women, white women, and so on).

19. Minority Women. In all programs recruiting or promoting minorities or women (or both), minority women must not be ignored. Minority women are also protected by legislation prohibiting discrimination on the basis of race.

20. Part-Time Status. HEW takes no stand. Women's groups recommend that part-time status be reevaluated. In some institutions, qualified faculty members can ascend the tenure ladder in part-time status.

21. In-Service Training. Training programs are suggested by HEW. All such programs are required to be open to persons of both sexes and all races.

22. Work Assignments. Teaching load, research responsibilities, and so on cannot be assigned on the basis of sex or race.

23. Termination and Reduction in Work Force. Disparate termination rates for women and minorities are prohibited unless the employer is able to demonstrate reasons unrelated to race, sex, national origin or religion. Lack of seniority cannot be used as a reason for termination when the person(s) laid off has been found to have less seniority because of previous discrimination.

24. Student Employment. Discrimination in employment of all staff, including undergraduate and graduate students is prohibited.

25. Publication of Affirmative Action Plans. Under the executive order, such plans, including numerical goals, must be disclosed (other than those parts which would involve confidential information about employees and would constitute a violation of privacy or would disclose financial information about the institutions).

myths and realities of affirmative action

Many of the issues of affirmative action now being debated somewhat *ex post facto* in the halls of ivy have already been decided in the courts. Court decisions that were previously applicable to discrimination in nonacademic settings now extend to the educational world. Thus the policies of affirmative action and numerical goals are not "diabolical" plans developed "conspiratorily" by HEW and other federal agencies. These concepts and precedents derive from statutes, legislative histories, judicial decisions, the principal of equity, and the Constitution. Civil rights legislation and court decisions, for example, are intimately related to the concept of *equity*: "setting things right." This is the guiding principle that underlies numerical goals. The Supreme Court has stated that the court "may order such affirmative relief as may be appropriate. [It] has not merely the power, but the *duty* to render a decree which so far as possible [will] eliminate the discriminatory effects of the past as well as bar like discrimination in the future" [Louisiana v. United States, 380 U.S. 145 (1965); Emphasis added].

Affirmative Action and Numerical Goals. The opponents of affirmative action often use the term *affirmative action* loosely and sometimes erroneously to describe a variety of actions. Broadly speaking, affirmative action consists of efforts aimed to end discrimination and to remedy the effects of past discrimination. It includes a great many activities which are not controversial, such as notifying women's and minority groups about job openings; advertising job openings rather than relying on word-of-mouth notification; developing recruiting procedures aimed at women and minorities as well as at other qualified applicants, and so on.

Of all the areas involved in affirmative action, the concept of numerical goals and timetables is perhaps the most controversial. Numerical goals are often confused with quotas; the terms are often erroneously used interchangeably. However, the government and the courts have made a clear distinction between the two: goals are legal; quotas clearly violate the Constitution and numerous federal statutes. Quota systems keep people out; goals are targets for inclusion of people previously excluded. *Goals are an attempt to estimate what the employer's work force would look like if there was no illegal discrimination based on race or sex.* Goals are aligned with the number or percentage of qualified women and minorities available and not in terms of their general representation in the population.

Under the executive order, the institution does its own analysis of its work force and determines if there is underutilization of women or minorities or both. For example, women receive about 23 percent of the doctorates awarded in psychology, and studies indicate that 91 percent of women with doctorates work. Furthermore, approximately 23 percent of the psychologists listed with the

National Register of Scientific and Technological Personnel are female. Thus if there were no women or substantially less than 23 percent women in a department of psychology, "underutilization" would exist. Such a presumption, based on statistical analysis, has been upheld in the courts. Indeed, statistics such as these can be used as *prima facie* evidence of discrimination. "Statistics often tell much, and the courts listen" (State of Alabama v. United States, 304 F. 2d 583 (5th Circuit 1962), *aff'd mem.*, 371 U.S. 37, 1962).

The courts have not hesitated to use statistics both as a measure of discrimination and as a measure of compliance. Institutions cannot rebut statistical evidence on the basis that no women or minorities applied. An institution may have a reputation as discriminatory, and that may have had a "chilling" effect on employment applications (Lea v. Cone Mills, 301 F. Supp. 97 (M.C.N.C. 1969); Cypress v. Newport News General and Non-Sectarian Hospital Assoc., 375 F.2d 648 (4th Cir. 1967)). Underutilization, under existing case law, raises a presumption of discrimination under the executive order and Title VII. When statistical evidence indicates that there has been a pattern of discrimination, the burden of proof is then shifted to the employer, who must then demonstrate that there is and has been no discrimination, that the job criteria are indeed job-related, and that employment practices do not and have not had a discriminatory effect.

Under the executive order, after an institution does its own analysis it sets its own goals, based on that analysis and subject to approval by HEW. Under Title VII, when a charge has been filed, EEOC does the analysis, and EEOC or the courts (or both) may set a goal upon a finding of discrimination.

Goals have been upheld in the courts as relief for a substantiated pattern of discrimination. (For a lengthy but only partial listing of cases, see *Technical Comment #1*, International Association of Official Human Rights Agencies, 1625 K St., N.W., Washington, D.C. 20006, September 7, 1972. When appealed to the Supreme Court, the Court has let these decisions stand by denying *certiorari*.) The aim is *not* punitive; no one is required to be fired. Goals are simply an attempt to remedy the continued effect of discrimination in the present and to give relief to a specific class that has been discriminated against in the past.

The goal is tailor-made to a specific situation, in terms of anticipated employee turnover rate, new vacancies, promotion and upgrading, and the availability of qualified women and minorities. The goal varies for different job classifications; it could be as general as one for "psychologists" or it could be more specific, such as one for "clinical psychologists." It will obviously vary for different job classifications; and within institutions, it will vary from department to department.

Preferential Treatment. Many people believe that goals and quotas are identical and that goals require preferential treatment. However, the courts have indicated that affirmative action in employment is legal and does not constitute preference when undertaken to remedy past discriminatory practices. Indeed, preference is clearly illegal under the executive order, Title VII [see section 703(j)], and all other laws requiring nondiscrimination. No institution is required to hire women or minorities on the basis of sexual or racial preference. To do so would clearly be illegal. Affirmative action is not aimed at creating preference but at *ending* the preference for white males which has always existed in academia.

What the executive order and Title VII do require is the obligation of fair recruiting and hiring. If an institution fails to meet the goals, it then has to show that it made a good faith effort to recruit, hire, and promote qualified women and minorities, and it has to be able to produce records documenting those efforts. For example, the department head may show that he or she has contacted women's groups (such as the women's caucuses relevant to the discipline), has contacted individual women scholars for referral of candidates, has included in letters to colleagues and in job advertisements statements like "women and minorities, including minority women, are welcome to apply" and has also evaluated those already in the department who might qualify for the opening. If, after doing all this, it turns out that all the women were poorly qualified, and the man hired was indeed the best qualified applicant, the employer can document a good faith effort at affirmative action and thus can justify the decision to hire the white male. If so, the employer has discharged the obligation under the executive order; the obligation to meet the goal is not absolute.

There is no requirement whatsoever that would force academicians to hire lesser qualified women or minorities. If the best qualified person is white and male, then that person can be hired. What the employer must be able to demonstrate is three-fold:

1. A genuine good faith effort to recruit women and minorities

(good faith does *not* mean calling one's white male colleague, asking if he knows a good *man,* and then, after the hiring is completed, saying: "Certainly I'd have been glad to hire a 'qualified' woman or minority person if I could have found one. Unfortunately, none applied.")

2. Specification of job-related objective criteria before the hiring process. The criteria for professional jobs are often complex and difficult to assess; nevertheless, they are subject to the same requirements as other jobs. Subjective, intuitive judgments are not acceptable criteria for hiring. For example, the courts have already held that promotional policies for executives are subject to standards of objectivity and must be job related (Marquez v. Ford Motor Co., Omaha District Sales Office, 440 F.2d 1157, 8th Cir., 1971).

3. Equal application of criteria. Whatever standards or criteria are set for white men must be applied equally to women and minorities.

In some instances, the courts have imposed a kind of limited preference–more stringent numerical goals than those required by institutions under the executive order. Court ordered goals have occurred only in public employment and industrial settings, not in academia.

The differences between court ordered goals and those required under the Executive Order are critical:

1. Under the executive order, goals are set by the institution, after it does its own analysis. In a court situation, the federal government does the analysis and sets the goal.

2. Under the executive order, the best-qualified person may be hired. Only in a court situation can a lesser qualified person be hired. This limited preference has been allowed in our courts only after a finding of discrimination, and for a limited time only. The affirmative action requirements that institutions voluntarily assume when they accept a contract, however, do not in any way allow or compel institutions to give preference to lesser qualified persons on the basis of race, color, national origin, or sex.

In the few cases where goals have been overturned by the courts, it was because the goal was not a goal but a quota, and because there was no provision to insure that qualified persons were hired. (See, for example, the 3rd Circuit decision overturning part of the order by the United States District Court in the Eastern District of Pennsylvania involving the hiring of policemen. Commonwealth of Philadelphia v. O'Neill, 5 EPD 1974: "This order does not, certainly on its face, limit the pool from which applicants are to be chosen to those necessarily qualified to be policemen.")

Is Preference Required by Law? Is Preference a Fact? Recently, there have been substantial questions raised about affirmative action and its implications for academia (Lester, 1974). Opponents of affirmative action claim that institutions are being "forced" to hire less qualified women and minorities and that institutions are giving preference in hiring based on sex and race. *Any institution that gives preference in hiring on the basis of sex or race or ethnic origin is violating the law.* Those that claim that they have been forced to give preference to lesser qualified women and minorities have sadly misunderstood the law and their rights under it.

The data concerning the increase in the hiring of women and minorities in academia simply do not uphold the academic myth that women and minorities are being hired in any great numbers by the academic community. A study at the University of Michigan of recent doctoral recipients showed that women doctorates were unemployed or underemployed at three times the rate of their male counterparts (School of Graduate Study, University of Michigan, 1974). In the biological and medical sciences, about 50 percent of the men who were in teaching institutions were in schools regarded as comparable to the University of Michigan; for the women, 16 percent were comparably placed.

Similar studies conducted within particular disciplines show the same pattern. The fear that unqualified women are invading the tenured ranks seems to have little basis in fact. Of nearly two hundred institutions with graduate programs in chemistry (which is virtually all of the institutions which have such programs), between 1971 and 1973, the increase in the number of women at the full professorship level was exactly *one.* At the associate professor level, a net gain of seven was reported. While it is true that the pool of women chemists is not very deep, there have been approximately fifteen hundred women who received Ph.D.'s in chemistry since 1960. Were there really only eight that were qualified to become associate or full professors in a two-year period? Somehow, women who are qualified to receive Ph.D.'s at our major institutions are "unqualified" to teach at those same institutions (Green, 1974).

The myth is that reverse discrimination is endemic and that white males are having difficulty because preference is being given to women and minorities. It is of course true that in a time of restricted budgets and a contracted economy it is harder for anyone, male or female, to find academic employment, but that is not reverse discrimination. Some of the complaints have been specious; several white men have complained of reverse discrimination simply because a woman was hired and they were not. The mere hiring of a woman, no matter how qualified, is assumed by some to be *prima facie* evidence of "reverse discrimination." In fact, the few women that have been hired have generally been superbly qualified.

While it is true that academic hiring has indeed slowed down, many institutions are still increasing their faculty, although at a far slower rate than previously. But few women and minorities are being hired, and when they are hired it is almost always at the lower ranks. The University of Minnesota, for example, reported that about half of its increase in academic staff consisted of white males. The women and minorities were hired in low positions, namely, part-time, on one year contracts, in instructorships, and the like. Only three of the fifty-three associate professor appointments were to women, and all three were either part-time or visiting appointments.

On occasion, some administrators have used affirmative action as an excuse for turning down applicants they did not want to hire. One department head at a large Western university wrote four of the five applicants for a position that he could not hire them because HEW insisted he hire a woman or minority. However, the fifth candidate—the one who got the job—was neither female nor minority; it was a white male. Needless to say, practices such as this violate the law, as well as generating inaccurate complaints of reverse discrimination.

On the other hand, some complaints of reverse discrimination have been justified. Some administrators have misunderstood the federal requirements and have erroneously believed that only women and minorities, including minority women, could be hired. HEW has played a major role in such misconceptions, and criticism of HEW for inefficiency, incompetency, and inconsistent interpretations is more than justified.

However, to confuse the incompetence of HEW with defects in the law itself would be tragic. It would be like saying that because some police are inefficient and incompetent, we should therefore abolish the laws they are supposed to enforce. Too often, there has been a vast difference between what the law actually requires and the lack of clear policies at HEW.

What some administrators object to most is the federal interference with the "traditional" methods of employment decisions in academia. No one wants the government to watch over their shoulder; but, on the other hand, it is difficult to justify why academia alone should be exempt from the same rules and regulations that apply to every other industry in the country. Any attempt to exempt academia from the federal regulations and statutes that prohibit discrimination would deprive women and minority faculty of the fundamental civil rights now enjoyed by all citizens of this country. It would be the first step backward in civil rights legislation, and it would set a dangerous precedent for other segments of society seeking exemption from these laws. Moreover, the Congress specifically rejected the notion that academic institutions should be treated separately from the rest of the country in 1972 when it amended Title VII of the Civil Rights Act of 1964 by deleting the exemption for educational institutions.

Administrators are understandably concerned about federal "interference" in hiring and promotion decisions. If an administrator or committee cannot justify a decision, then either someone is in the wrong job or getting the wrong salary, or else you have a very poor administrator or committee. Despite claims of an objective merit system, academic judgments in the past have too often been intuitive and subjective. Now instead of being able to justify a candidate merely by saying, "Dr. X is a fine fellow with a good reputation who has published a good deal," department heads will have to develop specific, objective criteria and be able to demonstrate that the candidate is the very best person recruited from the largest possible pool, a pool which will include qualified women and minorities. The demands of affirmative action, far from diminishing academic quality, are likely to increase it by requiring that hiring and promotion policies be truly based on merit without discrimination.

Institutions have generally relied on the "old boy" method of recruiting and hiring–the vast informal network of old school chums, colleagues, and drinking buddies–a network to which women and minorities rarely have access. The merit system has always been a closed merit system, for large portions of the available, qualified pool have been excluded. The government is not asking that the merit system be abolished, but only that it be opened to a larger pool of qualified persons. To recruit in a different manner means change, and change is never easy, particularly if it means women and minorities coming in to challenge the power base.

HEW, incidentally, does not set criteria for hiring and promotion; rightfully, that is a prerogative of the institution and its departments. What the government does ask is that the criteria be related to the job, and that institutions specify what the criteria are and how they are evaluated. No one is questioning the right and responsibility of the tenured faculty to recommend new appointments, reappointments, promotions, and salary increases. The government does not disturb this arrangement other than to ask that the persons making decisions be able to justify that those decisions were indeed made on the basis of quality and individual merit, and not based on any discriminatory factors. The justification of such decisions should not hamper the governance and decision-making traditions of academia; indeed it is far more likely to improve the quality of such decisions.

Many persons feel that the principles developed by the courts in industrial settings should not be applied to academia. While it is indeed true that academia is unique in many ways, it is indeed difficult to justify that employment in academia—other than in its decentralization—is markedly different from any other professional employment. Certainly, hospital clinics, law firms, top management in industry, and so on also want to hire the best qualified persons judged on the basis of professional competence. If the principles developed under our statutes and constitution are not applicable to academia, then what indeed would apply? Certainly the time-honored academic principle of hiring the best qualified on the basis of merit is not threatened by regulations which require exactly that: hiring the best qualified person on the basis of merit. Shall we exempt institutions from having to justify a hiring decision? Shall we exempt academic institutions from having criteria that are related to the job at hand and are not biased? Shall we exempt institutions from executive order requirements to do a self-study to uncover discrimination?

Dangers of Arbitration as a Proposed Solution. Many persons including Lester, are now promulgating binding arbitration as a way of handling academic discrimination. Such a procedure would have disastrous effects on the rights of women and minorities, for, typically, arbitration is not concerned with the principles of redress of grievances or inequities, but with working out a compromise position between two adversaries. The rights of the individual and due process are not essential to arbitration procedures; arbitrators are not required to follow federal standards or court derived principles in working out solutions. Thus an arbitration panel would not need to follow the definition of discrimination articulated by the Supreme Court in Griggs v. Duke Power Co., 401 U.S. 424 (1971). How would remedies be determined if the concept of equity is abandoned? What would be the standard of proof if there is no body of past decisions to fall back upon? Constitutional due process which is now assured in all forums involving discrimination would not be assured under arbitration. If, on the other hand, such concepts were incorporated by law into a binding arbitration process, then it is not clear how the arbitration process would be better than the conciliation process already available under Title VII. The Equal Employment Opportunity Commission requires that all complaints upon a finding of discrimination be conciliated. Should either party be unhappy with the conciliation proceedings, the courts are available. In contrast, any kind of binding arbitration would almost wholly bypass our court system and would probably rule out all class complaints and complaints concerning *patterns* of discrimination.

If the mediation-arbitration procedure was required of all academic discrimination complaints, it might well create a separate class of citizens: those with discrimination complaints in academia would have one set of procedures, and the rest of the country would have another. In effect, academic women and minorities, as well as academic men claiming reverse discrimination, would have less protection under arbitration than they do now. There would be no right of appeal nor any body of previous decisions to fall back upon. Moreover, unless the procedure was required by law, it might not be binding on women and minorities, for as the Supreme Court recently ruled in Alexander v. Gardner-Denver Co., a union contract requiring arbitration does not bar an employee from using Title VII machinery. Employees are not prohibited from filing charges of discrimination against their employer (or union) even if an arbitrator has rejected their claim. Thus, an employee is not bound to use the contract grievance machinery in instances involving discrimination, nor is the employee (in contrast to the employer) bound by adverse findings of an arbitrator. Justice Powell, who delivered the unanimous decision, stated that while the arbitrator's opinion may be entitled to some weight as evidence in the worker's Title VII claim, it was the federal courts and not the arbitrator that would have the last word.

Whether universities would agree to a procedure that is binding upon them but not on the grievant is questionable. Unless the grievant felt that he or she would get fairer treatment from the panel than from the courts, there might be little incentive to use it, particularly if the principles on which it would base its decision are unknown and likely not to be as beneficial (from the grievant's standpoint) as those that could be obtained by EEOC and the courts. While there might be economic incentives for a grievant to use the panel in preference to taking one's own suit to court, grievants now have the option of allowing EEOC to handle the complaint, with its power of requesting an injunction and using its own attorneys at no expense to the grievant in a court case. The large backlog in EEOC cases, however, might make the panel more attractive in terms of no backlog. (However, with 1,600 institutions charged under EEOC between 1972-1974, the panel might quickly run into the same backlog problem.)

Moreover, as well as individuals giving up their statutory rights, arbitration might also conflict with collective bargaining procedures: Individuals who were involved in union contracts would have to choose between their own required arbitration procedures and those set up for discrimination problems, or perhaps a person who simultaneously claimed discrimination and violation of union procedures would have two sets of arbitration proceedings to follow.

Among the advantages seen for the arbitration process is that lawyers are less likely to be involved and also that the confidentiality of records would be maintained. If the panel had any teeth, such as the power to grant tenure or back pay as a remedy, it is highly doubtful that either party would care to present their case without legal aid. Moreover, the issue of confidentiality, while understandably of great concern to institutions, is perhaps somewhat of a red herring. EEOC, under Title VII, is prohibited by law from releasing any information whatsoever concerning any case before them, including the names of either party to the complaint. The parties of the complaint, however, are not bound by this requirement. Should the case go to court, records can be made public, although either side could ask that the records be heard in camera. The Equal Pay Act is enforced with similar requirements of confidentiality; names and records are not released unless the case goes to court. Although the executive order has no such restrictions, HEW will not release any confidential records concerning individuals and is allowed to withhold these records under the Freedom of Information Act.

Institutions cannot on their own withhold such records from any government enforcement agency, but these records as mentioned above are indeed protected from public scrutiny (EEOC v. University of New Mexico, 7 EPD 9118, D. C., N. M., November 2, 1973).

Any type of binding arbitration procedure written into law to cover academics could open up a new series of court cases involving its relationship to Title IX, Title VII, The Equal Pay Act, Executive Order 11246, the Civil Rights Acts of 1866 and 1871 (Sections 1981, 1983 and 1985), and the Fifth and Fourteenth Amendments. Would the rights of individuals under those acts be suspended? Would women and minorities choosing an academic career have *less* or *different* rights from citizens choosing other types of employment?

conclusion

In summary, affirmative action is coming under a good deal of criticism, partly because it has been badly administered by HEW, and partly because some administrators in institutions of higher education have misunderstood the federal requirements. It would be tragic for the rights of citizens in this country if we confuse poor administration with imperfections in the law itself.

Yet at the same time that people are critical of HEW as being inconsistent and unable to understand academia, the same persons are recommending that there be only one single agency to deal with discrimination in academia and that that agency be HEW. Some women's groups interpret this as an indication that institutions would prefer HEW because it is most likely to be the weakest of all the enforcement agencies. Whether this be true or not is unclear; however, of all the agencies involved, HEW is most prone to respond to pressure from academic institutions. Women's groups are somewhat concerned about the rights of individuals in those circumstances. It is also important to note in this connection that the Congress in 1972 rejected the notion of any single mammoth enforcement agency for all discrimination complaints. A single enforcement agency would likely be far more rigid in requirements for institutions than is currently the case.

Moreover, the basic policies of the several agencies are remarkably similar: there are no conflicts, although the EEOC is somewhat stricter in its guidelines than those of the Departments of Labor and HEW in terms of pensions and maternity leave. However, any institution conforming to EEOC guidelines will be in compliance with those of the other departments.

Data collection is gradually being unified with the preparation of the new EEOC 6 form for educational institutions. Despite complaints, the collection of data is one of the unexpected benefits of government regulation: For the first time many institutions are collecting data that are not only necessary for affirmative action but are essential for effective fiscal planning and management. (For example, one of the most prestigious institutions in New York could not provide a simple list of all its personnel when asked to do so by HEW.) Such data, although sometimes expensive to collect initially, will repay costs as a result of better evaluation and planning on the part of institutions.

Despite all the complaints and criticisms, it is interesting to note that not one institution has ever had funds withdrawn or terminated because of discrimination. Not one institution has ever had new contracts delayed because of discrimination, although some institutions have had delays because of a lack of an affirmative action plan. Not one institution has ever requested a hearing under the executive order. Not one institution has ever had funds terminated, withdrawn, or delayed because of its failure to meet numerical goals. Not one charge of a pattern of discrimination filed with HEW has ever been refuted.

The academic community is one of the most powerful in this country—not because of money or direct power, but because it is responsible for training the youth and leaders of America. If women and minorities are to have the birthright that is that of their white brothers they must have the opportunity to partake in the fruits of higher education as students, as staff, as faculty, as administrators. To weaken *any* of the laws that protect them from discrimination, particularly those that affect education, would be a serious abrogation and denial of the rights of women and minorities.

The legislation that prohibits discrimination on the campus is very new. We had all hoped that with the passage of these laws that prohibited discrimination on the campus a new era had begun. But already, within a few short years the backlash has begun and attempts to weaken existing laws and regulations are well underway.

Women are the fastest growing, and potentially the largest, advocacy group on the campus, and, indeed, in the nation. No longer will they weep if they are denied the rights that are those of their brothers. For women have something else to do. They are learning the politics of change. They are learning that the hand that rocks the cradle can indeed rock the boat. And the campus, and the nation, will never be the same again.

references

Federal Laws and Regulations Concerning Sex Discrimination in Educational Institutions. Washington, D.C.: Project on the Status and Education of Women, Association of American Colleges.

Green, A. A. *Women on the Chemistry Faculties of Institutions Granting the Ph.D. in Chemistry.* Unpublished report by the Women Chemists Committee. Los Angeles: Immaculate Heart College, 1974.

Lester, R. *Antibias Regulations of Universities.* New York: McGraw-Hill, 1974.

School of Graduate Study. *The Higher; The Fewer.* Report and Recommendations of the Committee to Study the Status of Women in Graduate Education and Later Careers. Ann Arbor, Mich.: University of Michigan, 1974.

Bernice Sandler is executive associate and director of the Project on the Status and Education of Women at the Association of American Colleges. Formerly she was head of the Action Committee of the Women's Equity Action League (WEAL) which was instrumental in bringing about federal enforcement of Executive Order 11246 regarding sex discrimination in universities and colleges. She has served as a member of the Advisory Committee on the Economic Role of Women to the President's Council of Economic Advisors and in 1970 she was an education specialist on the staff of the special Subcommittee on Education of the House of Representatives, where she worked on the hearings on sex discrimination that laid the groundwork for Title IX and other legislation.

In this and the following article, two members of the Committee on Academic Nondiscrimination and Integrity raise objections to current federal affirmative action programs.

on discrimination: part one

sidney hook

My educational philosophy is derived from my teacher and friend, John Dewey, who taught that in a democracy every person has a right to that schooling which will enable him to achieve his maximum intellectual and spiritual growth as a human being, and that what intelligent and loving parents want for their children in the way of education, the community should want for all its children, regardless of race, religion, sex, or national origin.

Committed to this philosophy, I have fought all my life against all forms of invidious discrimination, especially in education. I have welcomed the long overdue Executive Order 11246 and its amendments as well as the Civil Rights Act of 1964. And it was this commitment that inspired my public criticism of the enforcement procedures of the Office for Civil Rights of The Department of Health, Education, and Welfare (HEW), delegated to it by the Department of Labor's Office of Federal Contract Compliance. For the directives and procedures that emanated from this office violated the spirit and letter of the executive order and the section 703(j) of Title VII of the Civil Rights Act of 1964, by requiring that "numerical goals and time schedules" be established to guide hiring practices of members of minorities and women wherever their underutilization is allegedly shown. In a series of articles, I developed the argument and showed that cognitively there was no difference between "good faith efforts" to achieve numerical goals within a certain time frame and "good faith efforts" to achieve quotas. Subsequently, I helped organize the Committee on Academic Nondiscrimination and Integrity, a group of distinguished scholars who are convinced that the educational health of the country, the public welfare, and plain justice require that appointments and promotions in the academy be determined solely on the basis of competence rather than by membership in any group; that academic integrity requires that the best qualified person be appointed to a post without consideration of scholastically extraneous factors such as race, sex, religion or national origin. Indeed, in behalf of the very principle that has inspired their opposition to past and present deplorable practices of discrimination *against* women and members of minority groups, the members of our committee are as steadfastly opposed to discrimination *in favor of* women and members of minority groups.

some peripheral questions

Do the Higher Education Guidelines of the Office for Civil Rights in effect call for or encourage preferential hiring or the introduction of a quota system as I maintained from the very outset of my criticism? Before considering this question, it is important to treat briefly some peripheral questions to avoid confusion.

We do not deny that discrimination in the past on grounds of religion, race, sex, and national origin has occurred, that in some places it still exists, and that it is morally wrong. We do not deny that this discrimination is apparent not only in hiring but in rewarding, promoting, and retiring, and that all such practices should be abolished forthwith. What makes these practices wrong is the violation of the merit principle. Individuals have been punished for no fault of their own but merely because they were members of some group, membership in which had nothing to do with the qualifications for the post in question. For the moment, I do not inquire whether purely statistical disproportions in the employment of individuals of various groups is cogent evidence of active discrimination.

Granted, then, the evil of past and present discrimination, what is the remedy? Surely not another kind of discrimination. No one would argue that because many years ago blacks were deprived of their right to vote and women denied the right to vote that today blacks and women should be compensated for past discrimination by being given the right to cast an extra vote or two at the expense of their fellow citizens or that some white men should be deprived of their vote. Take a more relevant case. For years blacks were shamefully barred from professional sports. Would it not be absurd to argue that therefore today in compensation for the past there should be discrimination against whites in professional athletics? Would any sensible and fair person try to determine what proportion of whites and blacks should be on basketball or football teams in relation to racial availability or utilization? We want the best players for the open positions regardless of the percentage distribution in proportion to ratios either in the general population or in the pool of candidates trying out. Why should it be any different when we are looking for the best qualified mathematician to teach topology or the best medieval philosophy scholar? Why not drop all color, sex and religious bars in honest quest for the best qualified, no matter what the distribution turns out to be? (The retort that dropping all bars of discrimination is not sufficient to achieve parity of representation for various groups is completely without merit since it assumes what has never been proved: that under fair and equal opportunities of vocational selection the ultimate outcome would reflect the proper proportions among qualified applicants.) Of course, the quest must be public and not only fair, but seen to be fair.

How can we drop all these extraneous, discriminatory bars and still strive to achieve "numerical goals"? If we abandon the discriminatory practices in recruiting, enrollment, salaries, and promotion, why do we need numerical goals unless it is argued that the only real proof of the abandonment is the achievement of these numerical goals?

"numerical goals" equals "quota"

The representatives of HEW shy away from the taboo word *quota* because they know that a quota system is incompatible with the basic norms of merit and individual justice. But a "numerical goal" when selections are guided by anything but merit is precisely what we normally mean by quota. In Europe the Latin phrase *numerus clausus* was used to set religious quotas for entry into universities. Where one says, "You are to aim at a quota of X percent of blacks, Chicanos, Puerto Ricans, women, and so on for your staff within two years," the meaning is the same as, "You are to set as your *goal* recruitment of X percent of blacks, Chicanos, Puerto Ricans, women, and so on within two years." The representatives of HEW confuse themselves and others by saying that numerical goals are not quotas because "good faith efforts" to achieve goals is "an adequate substitute for evidence that goals have been met." But this is logically equivalent to saying that sincere good faith efforts to achieve quotas are adequate evidence that quotas have been met. If anything is morally wrong, then sincere efforts to bring it about are wrong. If quotas are morally wrong in education, then sincere "good faith efforts" to achieve them are also wrong.

For some purposes (trade, immigration policy, rationing of scarce commodities, the compilation of jury rolls) a quota system may be legitimate and numerical goals reflecting a community's racial or sexual profile accepted as a guide. But when we are seeking the best qualified person or persons for a position, it is never morally legitimate to make membership in a group—whether religious, racial or sexual—a ground of selection, all the more so because such grounds of selection have been the cause of the discrimination in the past that we deplore.

When I first protested the establishment of numerical goals and timetables as part of the affirmative action programs demanded by HEW, I predicted that colleges and universities, in order to prove that they had made sincere, good faith efforts to achieve these goals, would resort to preferential hiring. That prediction has been fulfilled. The Anti-Defamation League, the University Centers for Rational Alternatives, and other organizations during 1972-73 have uncovered more than a hundred examples of racially determined preferential selection for 1972 and 1973. Even with our very limited resources hardly a day goes by in which we do not hear of continued discriminations. Many of the victims fear publicity.

The fundamental cause of this policy of discrimination, adopted presumably to end discrimination, is the requirement that numerical goals and timetables be an integral part of the affirmative action programs acceptable to HEW. Despite our repeated criticism, protestation, and petitions for the abandonment of prejudicial numerical goals and timetables, the Nixon administration refused to take any action. Yet these are the continuing source of preferential hiring practices. Where federal funds are necessary to the survival of so many institutions of higher education, administrators feel intimidated by the requirement. Representatives of HEW are confused by it themselves. One of them before the Special Subcommittee on Education of the House Educational Labor Committee on August 9, 1974, in answer to a question by Mr. Dellenback, concerning the degree to which numerical goals, at the end of a five year period, are to reflect the availability of minorities or women (or both), replied: "The OFCC regulations, in effect require that in the life of the plan, or the end of the life of the plan, the five years, that parity be achieved. If the work force is 20 percent female Ph.D., political science, one would expect that the composition of the faculty in X university would be 20 percent female" (Stenographic Transcript p. 296). And then, not having the courage of his confusions, he adds: "That is not a quota." But that it is a quota is apparent in the answer to Mr. Dellenback's next question: "What if a given institution . . . came to you with an affirmative action plan which showed very clearly that in solicitation, in hiring, and everything else that is followed thereafter, they really were on target in following the nondiscriminatory practice, they were really going to reach, but said nothing about what they would have in composition five years hence, would that be acceptable?" Mr. Holmes "No" (Hearings, p. 298).

Apparently then, absolute fairness in every aspect of the hiring, paying, and promoting process is *not* enough and the quota or goal *must* be reached. Despite this, Mr. Holmes then goes on to add, in reply to a further question: "We would urge the institution, as the regulations propose, that the goal be parity, but we will not, and we have not gotten hung up with an institution over that issue, if we think that the actions they are proposing to take are with regard to salary equity [equitable] and broadening [of] the recruitment process" (Hearings, p. 299). But if this is so then why require "numerical goals and time schedules," especially since they are the source, as HEW itself sometimes admits, of pervasive misunderstanding by university administrators?

conclusion

A few words in conclusion. Preferential hiring or quotas in education under any disguise is inherently divisive, unjust and undemocratic. It destroys the quest for excellence and opens the door to mediocrity injurious to students, educational institutions, and in the long run to the public good. It gives rise to the impression that even when inequalities and inequities in hiring practices, salaries, leaves, promotions, and tenure have been abolished, members of minority groups and women cannot make it on their own, that they require the crutch of extraneous group membership to compete successfully with others. It ultimately will be harmful to the professional dignity and integrity of all teachers, including those who slip into positions because they meet a quota or goal rather than because they have succeeded on merit. For it will create a two standard faculty—those who have made it on their own and those who have not. It tends to debase standards of scholarship and teaching under the cloak of combatting discrimination. Professor Jacob Neusner of Brown University is my authority for the following incident. I do not contend it is typical but it does point up a danger. Representatives of the Regional Offices of HEW demanded an explanation of why there were no women or minority students in the Graduate Department of Religious Studies. They were told that a reading knowledge of Greek and Hebrew was presupposed. Whereupon the representatives of HEW advised orally: "Then end these old fashioned programs that require irrelevant languages. And start up programs on relevant things which minority group students can study without learning languages."

If we are considering the question of quotas or any system of preferential selection in a larger context, it should be clear that it violates two fundamental and interrelated principles of social morality—justice and human welfare. Once basic human needs are equally gratified, differential rewards of scarce goods, services, and opportunities should depend upon merit or desert. The person who is best qualified for a post deserves it even if other considerations sometimes override his or her right. But, in this case considerations of human welfare strongly reinforce the right of award by merit because the consequences of recognizing it create values and goods that are to the benefit of the entire community. The principle of merit or desert therefore encourages and strengthens the quest for excellence. In the course of the pursuit of excellence everyone profits. In imposing a quota system we are not only defeating the ends of justice, but unnecessarily limiting multiple advances in human welfare. The society which today sacrifices the principle of merit and which downgrades the quest for excellence faces very bleak prospects of survival in our precarious and dangerous world.

In addition, the use of preferential treatment by race or sex, as a tool of the administration of social policy, presents the most dangerous kind of precedent to society at large. It not only sets groups against each other and promotes discord, but it also devalues what it means to be a citizen of the United States since what once was a precious right, equal justice under the law, becomes a privilege to be doled out at the pleasure of an administrator. Discrimination where it exists must and can be policed, punished, and eradicated, but it should not be created anew in the name of its opposite.

Our educational emphasis must fall not on lowering existing standards of achievement but on adopting all effective measures, financial, psychological, social, and pedagogical, that will increase the qualified supply of members of minorities and women. The community has a responsibility not only in education but in all areas of industry to provide employment for all who are willing and able to work. This expansion of opportunities on all levels of education does not require quotas or numerical goals but commitment to democracy as a way of life.

Sidney Hook, professor emeritus of New York University, is widely known for his philosophical, educational, and political thought as developed in Education for Modern Man, Political Power and Personal Freedom, *and* The Quest for Being. *He is a member of the Committee on Academic Nondiscrimination and Integrity. His recent testimony before the Special Subcommittee on Education of the House of Representatives, excerpted here, also appears in the September 1974 issue of* Measure, *the newsletter of the University Centers for Rational Alternatives.*

Suggestions for ending abuses of equal rights plans and implementing graded sanctions and appellate boards, from an able adversary of current programs.

on discrimination: part two

miro m. todorovich

For several years now, American colleges and university professors have found themselves psychologically squeezed between lofty egalitarian rhetoric and harsh realities of life. On the one hand, they are urged to work towards a fully nondiscriminatory society in which everyone will be treated "without regard" to race, sex, color, or national origin (Presidential Order 11246, Amended); on the other, regulations of the Department of Labor, the Department of Health, Education, and Welfare (HEW), and the Equal Employment Opportunity Commission (EEOC) demand that teachers and scholars become very much conscious of color, sex, and ethnos in dealing with all segments of their campus population and cooperate in the preparation of affirmative action plans, implying favored treatment of some groups designated as preferred. Members of our faculty are first told that it is up to them to develop sensible estimates of what can be reasonably accomplished; soon they find their institutions under the threat of governmental punishment if they do not conform to the demands of federal investigators. This enormous discrepancy between words and deeds, declared intentions and actual decisions of pertinent bureaucratic officials, can be illustrated by repeated factual examples.

the abuse of statistics

Affirmative action programs have fallen into abuses and contradictions essentially because their devisers sought to find a shortcut from the task of correcting the wrongs of discrimination. That shortcut was the so-called *statistical* method (usually characterized by a lack of statistical preparation) and it resulted in the goals and timetables. The problem arose that getting the proportions right is not the same thing at all as nondiscrimination. Looked at from the outside, from the point of view of a bureaucrat observing proportions, it may appear identical, but looked at from the inside, from the point of view of the man or woman, black or white, who has seen someone preferred to him or her precisely in *order* to get the numbers right, it is nothing more than discrimination in its crudest form. Like many shortcuts, this one turned out to be a snare and a delusion.

Not only have these programs worked injustice on many individuals and created a general cynicism about the justice of what should be merit considerations, but they are clumsy, expensive and time-consuming out of all proportion to their effectiveness, conceived in a spirit of *a priori* punitiveness, and, in short, unworkable. If many aspects of the regulations are meant to be taken at face value and their five or ten year deadlines enforced, it will be disastrous. If they are not meant to be enforced, then they represent a colossal waste.

The *numerical goals* and *precise timetables,* which seem to be the root cause of the new wave of discrimination and related malpractices, appear to have been created because they looked like the most convenient bureaucratic solution. The officials would not have to make the moral decisions involved in a finding of discrimination or its absence and they would not have to yield to the claims of professional competence made by those they were investigating and judging. All they would have to do would be to check off numbers on a list and think up requirements for others to fulfill. Once adopting this approach, the rule makers proceeded to devise orders, guidelines, and other ordinances while almost completely ignorant of the actual state of affairs in the professional labor market, of the statistical theory, and of the structure of educational institutions which they wanted to regulate. They never tried out a pilot project but rushed headlong into generalizations. They did not seek counsel from those ultimately involved in the programs, yet went forward with threats which touched upon the very financial survival of institutions under pressure. No wonder, then, that the consequences of such precipitous acts were both unpleasant and many and that one should now take decisive action to right the wrong.

Of greatest importance would be the dissociation of institutions of higher education from Department of Labor regulations which, even in their acceptable parts, reflect another domain of applicability and are poorly suited for institutions of higher learning. Also, the demands for numerical goals and timetables should be rescinded in the light of their proven ineffectiveness on the one side, and their inordinate cost and enormous potential for harm on the other.

This would pave the way for the development by appropriate groups of experts under the overall supervision of the Department of Health, Education, and Welfare of a new set of antidiscrimination rules, implementing the pertinent statutes, which would be fair, just, equitable and workable.

suggestions for action

The following suggestions might be useful in formulating an approach that places the best of the present collection of programs into the context of a genuine nondiscrimination plan.

1. Colleges and universities should be asked to comply with clearcut nondiscrimination directives in the areas of recruitment, hiring, promotion, retirement, salary, and adjudication of grievances. These would reflect the spirit as well as the letter of Executive Order 11246, which seeks to cast the net as widely as possible for all qualified applicants for a position and to guarantee that all are treated "without regard" to their race or sex. Such directives clearly would have to preclude the existence of any double standard, either substantive or procedural. There would be no room for such exercises as the newly stated hiring policy of the chancellor of the State University of New York. This policy requires voluminous documentation if a white male is to be hired, including letters of disinterest from women and members of designated

minorities invited to consider job offers, and often already holding other jobs. On the other hand, if a member of one of the preferred groups is to be hired, comparatively little paperwork is required. Such a policy discourages the hiring of qualified white males just as surely as grandfather clauses and poll taxes once discouraged voting by blacks. Such differential approaches, if accepted for use against any group can be used against all.

2. Antidiscrimination directives applicable to educational institutions should be the joint product of educators and government officials aided by statistical and other experts. In the future there should be much greater cooperation between bureaucrats and academics on projects of common concern. An office in HEW, centralizing the development and oversight of affirmative action programs in education, should be staffed by personnel which is substantially more knowledgeable about the nature of universities than was the case in the past. This may bring to an end many of the complaints heard from university administrators and faculty about the unreality of bureaucratic programs.

3. Educational autonomy should be strongly reaffirmed in the fields of curriculum, staffing, and teaching. The attempts by government officials to interfere with academic structures and content out of a desire to facilitate the fulfillment of the programs they oversee is one of the more alarming side effects of the present melange of programs. Government officials are there to see that discrimination is halted, not to determine teaching qualifications, course requirements, or academic standards. As a corollary, one would expect that overall governmental intervention would be held at a minimum compatible with the actual task at hand.

4. A limit should be set on the time a bureaucratic agency may take in considering a submitted plan. At present, years can go by without word from the federal government on whether or not a plan has been accepted. This procedural custom has the substantive effect of transforming the judicial function of bureaucrats into a tormenting and harassing one, since one's case is always pending before a judge who at the same time sends his emissaries to make further demands. If such a time limit were to be passed, the submitted plan should, like a Congressional bill, be considered accepted.

The power to deprive a university of funds should not be given to any official graced with a telephone and an intention to do so. A breathing space should be required before any funds are cut off. The regulations should provide for a reasonable and sufficient amount of time for the university to discuss and appeal the administrative decision.

5. A system of graded sanctions should be adopted to punish breaches of obligations in various degrees, as proposed by Professor Jan Vetter of the Berkeley Law School in a report prepared for the Administrative Conference of the United States ("Affirmative Action in Faculty Employment Under Executive Order 11246"). The conference has not acted on or adopted this report as yet. The either/or of cutting off federal funding is an exceptionally clumsy way of meting out punishment. If the NCAA can control its member colleges through graded sanctions, it is hard to see why the United States Government cannot.

6. The present practice that essentially the same group of officials produces regulations, investigates their application, passes judgment on possible noncompliance, metes out punishment, and dictates the remedies should be abolished and the various functions should be vested in mutually independent entities. In particular, the determination of institutional noncompliance and the subsequent imposition of sanctions should be done by forums (commissions, tribunals, boards of inquiry and the like), which would include distinguished and knowledgeable members of the academic community.

7. The present requirement of affirmative action programs that colleges and universities maintain effective and reliable grievance procedures should be retained. But there is no sense in mandating such programs if it is not also mandated that they be used.

Such a system of grievance proceedings throughout academia may do much to deal with the complaints of discrimination that do arise. Of course, it is understood that there should be an appellate system outside the given institution to which unsatisfied grievants may bring their case. Such an appellate system should be the heart of a genuine antidiscrimination program. It would not be hard to establish impartial boards of expert professionals to decide cases of discrimination in institutions not their own. Such boards could be set up in any number of ways. One possibility would be for the professional associations to develop lists of professionals willing to serve, on retainer, on such boards. The plaintiff and the defendant could each choose representatives from them to form an appellate board. The boards could either operate autonomously, under the aegis of federal officials who would make sure that the law was not broken, or as part of the federal enforcement system. In that case, the government could either select its expert for the board or even send its own representatives to serve as chairman or chief ombudsman. The funding for this program would be trifling compared to the present expenses of arranging, complying, and policing compliance with the unattainable goals and timetables.

The obvious and overwhelming advantage of these boards is that they would be competent and designed to deal with individual cases of discrimination as they occur to individuals wherever and whoever they may be. Whereas now only certain groups (identical with those thought relevant to the Philadelphia construction industry) are scouted for "underutilization" under this plan discrimination against ethnic Catholics, Sephardic Jews, the physically handicapped, or anyone else, could be ferreted out and rectified. Administrative judges would not have to avoid discussion of the merits of the case because of professional incompetence or ignorance, though confidentiality should be maintained outside the hearing.

One could anticipate two major objections to this plan. The first is that the number of cases is so enormous that they cannot be dealt with on an individual basis. The second objection is that it would require an agreement to allow these appellate hearings to be final and that neither the bureaucracy or the courts should be allowed to grant *de novo* trials.

It is simply not true that such boards would be swamped with cases. The prime piece of evidence for the belief that they would be is the failure of the EEOC to cope with its enormous backlog of cases. However, of those hundreds of thousands of cases, only about sixteen hundred stem from postsecondary education, of which not all were faculty cases. In addition, the EEOC, with its limited number of regional offices, does not, in resolving these cases, have a large enough staff which could come close to replacing, either in knowledge or in number, the many independent experts who would work on all campuses. It should also be noted that the disposition of cases involving New York University before the various boards in New York City and New York State, indicates that all thirty-four of the charges dealt with up to now turned out to be unjustified or were withdrawn. It is therefore only reasonable to predict that only a relatively small number of cases would remain active and perhaps travel all the way down the appellate road. Thus there is every reason to assume that a cooperative program, uniting government and academic forces, could easily cope with the complaints of discrimination, where the wholesale punitive measures used at present merely create additional cases of discrimination.

The second objection has two parts. Would the agencies and would the courts cooperate? Under this plan, the joint government-academic boards could easily *be* the agency grievance scheme, whether involving HEW or EEOC or some other governmental agencies. But certainly there should be no level of agency appeal above these boards. As far as the courts are concerned, the right to a trial *de novo* presumably cannot be challenged by either the executive or legislative branches and thus a disappointed plaintiff could still go to court under this plan. However, he or she can do so now. (The plaintiffs whose cases were dismissed in the NYU case have not all plunged into litigation. After losing twice, on the merits, not everyone remains unconvinced. It is unlikely that universities would frequently go to court in such circumstances). It would thus be a very curious argument which saw in the fact that trials *de novo* are available to citizens unsatisfied with internal or agency grievance proceedings, an argument for abolishing any and all such procedures.

It is very unfortunate that to a large extent the present difficulties may have originated from a spirit of implacable mistrust which expresses itself in the belief that no group of expert academics can be trusted to be fair to women and minorities. In truth, however, this objection is without merit. The very fact that the HEW guidelines speak of remedying underutilization and not of correcting discrimination, indicates that the problem all along has been for universities at the graduate level a question of inadequate supply. The absence of substantial pools of unemployed women and minorities substantiates this. For example, even the discrepancy between the 5.2 percent unemployed women versus 1.1 percent unemployed men in physics achieves its true proportions when we reflect that it involves a total discrepancy of exactly twenty jobs, a truly insignificant number when compared to the number of physics departments in this country. Even where it can be presumed that there is a department or dean that discriminates or would like to, on the basis of race, or sex, or religion, or national origin, it is wholly unrealistic to think that among the range and scope of

American academics none can be found who will be fair to a complainant. The recent responses of the professional associations to the problem of pension benefits and the allocation of scholarships, confirm the exact opposite of this cynical belief.

The thoroughgoing suspicion that refuses to cooperate with those who are to be regulated and which seeks to treat them as guilty in principle cannot possibly lead to nondiscrimination in an area in which so much depends on considerations of professional merit as judged by peers. It is absolutely necessary for the future that regulations be proposed, discussed, and adopted in a spirit of openness, mutual respect, and cooperation, and not imposed arbitrarily and in ignorance from above.

Miro M. Todorovich, associate professor of physics at Bronx Community College of the City University of New York, acts as coordinator for the Committee on Academic Nondiscrimination and Integrity and serves on the editorial board of Measure, *the newsletter of the University Centers for Rational Alternatives.*

The issues in expanding employment opportunity for women and minorities from the perspective of a federal "enforcer," the Director of the Office for Civil Rights of the Department of Health, Education, and Welfare.

affirmative action: myth and reality

peter e. holmes

In a lecture delivered at Andover Academy before becoming Ambassador to India, Daniel P. Moynihan told his audience that clues to America's future are now more likely to be found by reading Balzac than Mark Twain. "Find out," he said, "what it's like to live in a society where, if you want to be a professor, you wait until the man who is professor dies. Then the fifteen of you who want the job compete in various ways. One of you gets it. The rest hope for the best for their sons."

Moynihan went on to remark that there were students at the Graduate School of Education at Harvard who were finding it rough to locate a job. Evidently, during the current decade, no *new* school teachers will be needed, provided that the present student-teacher ratio is maintained. During the 1960s, the youth group fourteen to twenty years old grew by 13.8 million or 52 percent—five times the average decade rate of the preceding seventy years. After this unique jump, only eleven percent increase is forecast for the 1970s.

In short, indications are that the country has reached an end to the fantastic growth rate of the university community.

Needless to say, such a situation does not bode well for those of us who are concerned with expanding employment opportunity for women and minorities. For, although the obligation to take affirmative action will accelerate gains in this area, regardless of the total number of faculty positions, such gains may well be less than spectacular. Moreover, the anticipated letup in the expansion of faculty employment rolls suggests that public concern about the essence and impact of affirmative action is likely to persist.

Basically, affirmative action is a commitment to find means of providing access to opportunities heretofore denied to certain individuals or classes of individuals (or both). Controversy about this commitment first erupted in the pages of *Commentary* when Professor Paul Seabury of the University of California at Berkeley warned that "a new hidden crisis of higher education is brewing" (*Commentary,* February 1972). About the same time the *New York Times* ran an editorial sympathetic to Seabury's point of view, criticizing the Department of Health, Education, and Welfare for demanding access to personnel files and claiming that a resort to "quotas" was the "unmistakable suggestion in HEW's approach." (*New York Times,* March 2, 1972). The issue was joined.

At the Office for Civil Rights at HEW, which is charged with the responsibility of enforcing the affirmative action standards of Executive Order 11246, controversy has long been a way of life. Following passage of the Civil Rights Act of 1964, and the subsequent organization of a separate office at HEW to administer Title VI of that statute, public interest in school desegregation seldom flagged. One got used to reporters, as well as to press articles which more than once painted a less than fully authentic picture of events. But all this was important in bringing to bear upon the issue of school desegregation a continuing focus which made possible a swell of fairly well-informed public opinion.

We feel confident that public debate will continue to have a similar redeeming influence with respect to the issue of affirmative action, even though what appears in the media may often distort the true picture or lend credence to simplistic notions. In many respects our relationships with universities have improved over the course of the past year, generally because fundamental prerequisites in developing an acceptable affirmative action posture have taken hold and jointly we have been able to contend with and surmount some of the threshold obstacles, both practical and philosophic. However, there remain widespread misconceptions rooted in the early public record which are still given currency and which continue to mar progress.

I propose to explore some of these popular misconceptions, not for the purpose of reinvigorating still lingering conflicts of opinion but in order to give what I hope will be a helpful perspective to our office's approach in enforcing the law.

clarifying the issues

In meeting its responsibility to answer objections and to discuss with affected institutions their apprehensions about affirmative action, the Office for Civil Rights has sought to clarify the basic requirements imposed. Essentially, each university that is a federal contractor or subcontractor must analyze its work force to identify any practices that serve to deny to women and minorities equal pay, equal privileges, and an equal opportunity for employment and promotion. Universities must also identify conditions of "underutilization" of women and minorities and take steps, including the development of realistic goals and timetables, to correct such conditions. All universities subject to the executive order must develop and implement an affirmative action plan designed to overcome discrimination and "underutilization." The drafting of such a plan requires that institutions obtain and continually update personnel information such as the race, sex, and job classification of academic and nonacademic employees.

Finally, the federal government has the authority to cancel contracts and terminate eligibility for contract awards with respect to institutions that fail to comply with equal employment opportunity requirements subject, of course, to fair hearing procedures. In certain instances, the federal government also has the authority to delay or to deny the award of specific contracts when the facts indicate that the prospective contractor will not be able to comply with the requirements, which form a part of the contract.

To most people, all of this sounds eminently reasonable. Even those persons who have been most vocal in their opposition to the implications of the affirmative action principle have freely acknowledged that at many institutions, the traditional means of filling vacancies often acted to limit or exclude consideration of qualified women and minorities.

However, in itself the obligation to open the university employment process to federal scrutiny, and to widen its scope to include additional potential sources of talent, was enough to put us at odds with many well-intentioned critics.

For example, Mr. Seabury claimed that the so-called "best" universities which he did not identify but which presumably include the Berkeley campus, "habitually and commonsensically recruit from the best institutions." Affirmative action was seen to threaten such inbreeding. By implication, to reach outside this ambit for qualified candidates would ultimately serve to undermine an institution's legitimate effort to preserve and improve the quality of its faculty.

No one, however, quarrels with the right of one of Mr. Seabury's "best" institutions to recruit from the ranks of their brethen. And such an alliance is not, standing alone, what HEW is objecting to. Rather, the principle of affirmative action is that if the traditional recruitment process fails to yield qualified women and minority candidates, a university should seek to broaden that process by attempting to reach *additional* sources of qualified applicants—not by *abandoning* existing sources deemed by an institution to constitute a reliable skill pool. That such an amended process could lead, in Professor Seabury's words, to a situation where "quality must in fact be jeopardized" has not been empirically demonstrated.

The underlying assumption of affirmative action is that qualified women and minority applicants for faculty positions exist and that, as federal contractors, universities must give them an equal opportunity to compete for those positions by eliminating practices which realistically have foreclosed their candidature in significant numbers in the past. To conclude that on this basis affirmative action represents an assault on merit is to impart to qualified potential applicants who are other than white and male a stigma of professional inferiority which is not sustainable. Secondly, to infer that by requiring an expansion of the applicant pool, HEW is also requiring the employment of persons who are considered less qualified than other applicants, in order to fulfill a hiring goal, represents a distortion unsupported by the governing regulations.

To be sure, an institution which falls short of meeting a realistic hiring goal that forms part of an affirmative action plan must be able to document the efforts it has made to recruit qualified women and minorities. To some, measuring such "good faith" efforts to carry out the plan in any particular circumstance is like groping in the dark and is bound to bring about countless arbitrary decisions on the part of government functionaries. Yet it is plain enough that this standard affords to a university the widest scope to make employment decisions according to its own sense of mission and priorities, as long as the criteria applied are not discriminatory. Far from being a concept likely to be detrimental to the university and subject its hiring decisions to a new set of professional qualifications promulgated by Washington, the concept of good faith demands no more than that the university define and justify the standards it applies and the decisions that are reached as a consequence.

Assuming in the first instance that the government has a legitimate interest in assuring that its contractors correct practices which tend to limit or exclude the employment or promotion of women and minorities, on the basis of statistical evidence indicating that such lack of opportunity has in fact prevailed in the past, there must be means to weigh the extent to which contractors are carrying out their obligation if that obligation is to amount to more than a paper commitment.

To charge the contractor with the responsibility to demonstrate good faith efforts to recruit and employ women and minorities strikes a balance between the public interest in breaking with the trends of past injustice on the one hand, and the interest of the contractor in seeking to preserve valid academic standards.

Further, to argue that demonstrating good faith efforts is a burden that no institution will be able to sustain is to suggest at the same time that hiring decisions are based on criteria unfathomable to the non-academic mind, that no justifiable criteria exist, or that a university's prized defense of and search for merit is nothing but a chimera.

The affirmative action process is most certainly not anti-merit; it assumes the right of an institution to hire and promote persons who are deemed most qualified. But those who oppose affirmative action on grounds that it will chip away at standards of merit cannot in the same breath dispute the test of good faith, for to do so is to admit that the very standards felt to be threatened are impossible to define, and if they are impossible to define, one must wonder how universally applicable they are in the university community.

"revised order no. 4"

Mr. Seabury's article and the questions it raised proved to be but the tip of an iceberg. A year later, excerpts from a report to the American Association of Presidents of Independent Colleges and Universities were reprinted in a popular newsweekly (*U.S. News and World Report,* January 1, 1973). In this report the Office for Civil Rights was accused of "developing enforcement procedures which reflect a political attempt to mold the hiring practices of America's colleges and universities." Here, as elsewhere, the lore of government bureaucracy on the move against meritocracy found support, or so it seemed, in an amendment to the pertinent federal regulation published on December 4, 1971 (41 CFR Part 60-2). That amendment, commonly known as "Revised Order No. 4," sets forth specific guidelines for the development and implementation of acceptable affirmative action plans and formed the basis for HEW's own "Higher Education Guidelines under Executive Order 11246," issued in the fall of 1972.

Section 60-2.24 (f)(5) of the Revised Order No. 4 reads as follows:

> (f) The contractor should insure that minority and female employees are given equal opportunity for promotions. Suggestions for achieving this result include:
>
> (5) Make certain "worker specifications" have been validated on job performance related criteria. (Neither minority nor female employees should be required to possess higher qualifications than those of the lowest qualified incumbent.)

Typically, this section of the regulation was seized upon in the above-mentioned report, and in other forums, in the context of discussing the impact of affirmative action on hiring decisions.

Yet the language of Section 60-2.24 (f) clearly states that it is addressed not to hiring policy but to promotion policy, and that the subsections constitute not requirements but suggestions.

We construe the sections as prohibiting a contractor's use of an unnecessarily high standard of qualification intended or serving to exclude women and minorities from promotion consideration at a higher rate than others. Clearly, the object in mind is to discourage contractors from applying an abnormally rigorous standard in order to exclude or limit persons from consideration on a racial or sex basis. This does not, however, require the employment or promotion of a person solely because that individual meets the qualifications of the least qualified incumbent, and the sections do not so provide.

the chimera of federal harassment

A recurrent theme found in articles about affirmative action is the notion of the heavy hand of government, primed to pounce with a certain glee on institutions for the least offense. The requests of HEW to undertake corrective action on the basis of on-site reviews, and to implement effective affirmative action plans consonant with Department of Labor regulations, are perceived by some persons as dictatorial decrees thinly, if not overtly, akin to the worst features of an overweening federal presence. In this scenario a handful of middle grade compliance officials are threatening to take control over "admissions, hiring, curriculum, and campus policy" and institutions are "assumed guilty until proven innocent" (excerpts of report to American Association of Presidents of Independent Colleges and Universities, printed in *U.S. News and World Report,* January 1, 1973). Instances in which HEW has taken steps resulting in the temporary suspension of new contract awards are commonly looked upon as harassment.

The truth of the matter is that, in the five years since compliance activity was initiated in 1968, not one administrative enforcement proceeding has been carried through against a university with a view to debarring the institution from receiving federal contracts. Because of limited staff resources, the Office of Civil Rights has not yet been able to conduct comprehensive on-site compliance reviews of the vast majority of non-construction contractors under our jurisdiction. Regrettably, also, numerous class action complaints are still pending investigation and in other cases we have not been able to review and resolve individual complaints in a timely manner. Finally, the executive order and its implementing regulations, pertaining to equal employment opportunity, do not convey authority to willy-nilly dictate student admission or curriculum changes at colleges and universities.

Confusion has arisen particularly in the context of the Government's authority to postpone a contract award or, in other words to delay a final decision as to the contractor's eligibility for the award until further pertinent information is developed.

Under existing procedures, the Office for Civil Rights is routinely contacted by the Government contracting officers whenever a contract award of $1 million or more is pending. (It should be noted that while the focus here is on contracts of $1 million or more, any bidder for a federal contract of over $10,000 must be able to comply with the executive order.) Our role in such situations is to give the contracting officer advice as to whether the contractor-bidder is able to fulfill the equal employment opportunity requirements. The Office for Civil Rights will answer in the negative under the following conditions:

1. When a compliance review reveals that a contractor-bidder is not in compliance with the executive order because of a failure to have an acceptable affirmative action plan or because the contractor-bidder has substantially deviated from the approved plan. (Under this particular circumstance, the contractor-bidder may avoid a determination that it is non-responsible only if it can otherwise be affirmatively determined that the contractor-bidder is able to comply or the Director of the Office of Federal Contract Compliance, Department of Labor, finds that a hearing is necessary prior to making such a determination.)

2. When, following a compliance review, a contractor-bidder has failed to make commitments to correct equal employment deficiencies noted during the review.

3. When an "affected class" problem has been identified and the contractor-bidder has failed to develop corrective action.

There may be other clear-cut cases as well where HEW will determine that a contractor-bidder is unable to comply with the executive order and is therefore not a "responsible" contractor-bidder.

In the case of pending contract awards of $1 million or more, the Office for Civil Rights, pursuant to Department of Labor regulations, has 30 days in which to determine whether the contractor-bidder is able to comply with the Executive Order. It may be necessary to extend this period because, prior to conveying to a contracting officer information as to whether the contractor-bidder is able to comply, we must be able to assure that the contractor-bidder was provided ample opportunity to comply or to refute the assertion of noncompliance. As a practical matter, the Department's burden of being able to demonstrate efforts to secure voluntary compliance, coupled with the time constraints placed on contracting officers in making final decisions on contract awards, has thus restricted the circumstances under which our office has been able to declare contractor-bidders non-responsible. Records show that contract awards were postponed or delayed in only 16 cases since compliance activity commenced in 1968.

We are now in the process of defining more carefully the conditions under which HEW compliance officers will convey information which may lead to the denial or delay of a contract award. Also, if and when additional staff positions requested in the fiscal year 1974 budget become available, the new resources will help implement pre-award responsibilities in a more effective and comprehensive manner.

What must be clear from this brief summary is that there are practical constraints to the authority of a compliance agency such as the Office for Civil Rights to take steps resulting in the denial or delay of the contracting process, and that these constraints must be balanced against the obligation to assure that contracts are not awarded to nonresponsible contractor-bidders. For obvious reasons, we have been conscious of the need to assure that at every turn the particular measures undertaken or recommendations submitted are legally sound. Far from applying sanction, penalties, and threats in such a manner as to constitute what some might regard as an abuse of power, the comparatively few cases in which the Office for Civil Rights has prompted the delay of contract awards is evidence enough of our continuing endeavor to provide the higher education community with every opportunity to meet its obligations. And while HEW has dispatched notifications to a number of institutions indicating that enforcement action would be undertaken in the event the institutions persisted in a failure to correct deficiencies, submit an adequate plan, or provide access to relevant employment data, such action was taken only after prolonged and ultimately fruitless discussions in which every opportunity to voluntarily comply with clear regulatory provisions was provided.

Indeed, one might say that it is precisely the length of time afforded to institutions to reach a posture of compliance with Department of Labor regulations that has provoked, on the other side of the aisle, persistent criticism that HEW is not enforcing the law, or at least is not doing so with that display or notorious zeal alleged in some university circles. If to Professor Sidney Hook, formerly of New York University, HEW's requests to comply with affirmative action requirements are as offensive as "illiberal ultima" (*New York Times,* November 5, 1971), they are lame and entirely too scarce among groups of women and minorities who still see in the laws and authorities made for their protection an unfilled promise.

Dr. Bernice Sandler, the Director of the Project on the Status and Education of Women, Association of American Colleges, has testified that "(The) long delay in investigation and conclusion (of executive order complaints and reviews of affirmative action plans) not only contravenes federal policy and denies women their rights, it also harms institutions. Many women discouraged and embittered by lack of HEW action, have now taken their cases to court . . . It is clear that the enforcement of the executive order by OCR has been far from adequate" (Testimony before the Joint Economic Committee, July 11, 1973).

Here again, it should be understood that in the pleas of women's organizations we find areas of agreement. Frequently, the Office for Civil Rights has become involved in too many simultaneous commitments, impairing our ability to resolve pending cases expeditiously. Then too, the interpretation of regulations and their application to academic employment has imposed upon us, as well as upon colleges and universities, a process of learning in which mistakes have been and no doubt will continue to be made.

Since fiscal year 1972 the Office for Civil Rights has had a complement of only 80 professional and clerical staff assigned to executive order compliance in this field—much too small for the enormous job entailed in carrying out a program which was constantly being refined in the form of revised regulations. Understandably, as regulations were issued, and as the Office for Civil Rights proceeded to draft its own "Guidelines" specifically geared to university employment, the task of developing in-house the necessary skills to carry out the law has cut into time that might otherwise have been devoted to compliance activity.

But criticism from this quarter should not lead one to suppose that enforcement of the executive order has not left its mark on the employment practices of colleges and universities. Clearly, university administrators are today much more keenly aware of their affirmative action responsibilities than they were a bare three years ago. Last December, for instance, my predecessor at the Office for Civil Rights reported on a survey undertaken at 29 institutions in the states of Oklahoma, Texas, New Mexico, Louisiana, and Arkansas where HEW had undertaken compliance activity. The results of the survey indicated a marked increase in the number of minorities and women employed in managerial, professional, technical, clerical, and craftsman positions.

Equally or more important, as I shall point out, were indications received by our regional offices at the time that colleges and universities were moving to correct certain practices in areas such as promotion and pay that had served to deny to individual women and minorities an equal opportunity to compete and to advance within the system. Such indices of progress, although still slight, do not often get into public print where, alternately, the Government's efforts to enforce the law are all too frequently pictured as woefully inadequate or affirmative action itself is viewed as an anti-egalitarian scheme that can only destroy academic freedom.

equality of treatment or preferential treatment

Those who take the latter position invariably point to what they regard as a perverse anomaly: namely, that the government, in seeking to interpret and apply laws and authorities designed to end discrimination, is in fact mandating or authorizing the adoption of measures that have the opposite effect.

In this vein, special efforts to recruit and promote qualified women and minorities are seen to conflict in practice with the executive order's mandate to treat everyone equally, without regard to race, color, religion, sex, or national origin. In other words, affirmative action gives a "preference" to persons on the basis of factors which really shouldn't have a bearing at all.

However, the first thing that must be understood is that the executive order assumes that some persons, on the basis of their affiliation with a certain identifiable class or group, have been underrepresented, underpaid, and disadvantaged relative to other persons not so affiliated. Second, that because of this historical problem, affirmative steps are necessary to bring about equality of treatment, steps that go beyond a mere passive neutrality and verbal assurances of good conduct. What some might call an unlawful "preference" instilled by affirmative action is in fact an employment posture designed in time to shed preference—an employment posture that serves, by means of self-evaluation and commitment, to rectify conditions of inequality. Finally, affirmative action must also be understood as a vehicle to help minimize the potential for discrimination in light of past practices.

Nevertheless, in support of the theory that affirmative action demands illegal and self-contradictory "preference," publicists lean heavily on examples of cases in which institutions, or departments of instruction have evidently misconstrued the affirmative action obligation by allegedly instituting ad hoc procedures which served to discriminate against males and nonminorities. Generally, it is intimated that HEW perpetrates, encourages, or condones such practices, or is quite content to look the other way. Routinely, readers are left with the mistaken impression that aberrant measures taken in the name of affirmative action which violate the executive order are the wave of the future, that they express the program's ultimate silent purpose, and that they will spread like some cancer to all institutions of learning unless the country's true liberals wake up to the disaster just around the bend.

Thus, in characteristic fashion, Dr. John H. Bunzel, president of California State University at San Jose, pays due respect to equal opportunity but quickly notes in the same paragraph of a recent article that he is "opposed to the use of any form of quota system." Inasmuch as this steadfast opposition is expressed in the context of berating HEW for making of affirmative action "one of the most divisive issues in American higher education, and possibly one of the most anti-intellectual," lay readers are led to identify HEW as the culprit behind the imposition of hiring quotas ("The Politics of Quotas," *Change* Magazine, October 1972).

The Office for Civil Rights joins Dr. Bunzel and his associates in condemning illegal hiring quotas. However, we dispute the inference that goals are by definition quotas, that the distinction is simply a matter of semantics, and that HEW is applying otherwise legitimate principles in a discriminatory manner.

Dr. Bunzel proceeds to cite an instance where a university department apparently rejected a candidate on grounds of race and attributes such discrimination not to the lack of judgment of the department in question but to the perfidious consequences of officially inspired affirmative action, as if an intelligent reading of applicable regulations could actually lead one to conclude that such practices are lawful. To Professor Hook, this kind of documentation establishes beyond doubt that institutions are "knuckling under to the demands of HEW"; it is Professor Hook's thesis that these "demands" amount to a requirement to shun the best qualified person in favor of employing persons solely on the basis of race or sex. The trend is "continuing apace," he reports ("Semantic Evasions," *Freedom at Issue,* July/August 1972, No. 14).

That there have been excesses, masking as legitimate affirmative action, is indisputable. And, in full recognition of the fact that the law does not distinguish degrees of discrimination in terms of the affected group, and that it is our obligation to act to eliminate discrimination when allegations are brought to our attention to the extent resources and pending commitments permit, the Office for Civil Rights has reviewed the apparent existence of improper practices or activities at 30 institutions of higher education. In most cases, the institution or department apparently acted to reserve positions exclusively for female or minority candidates, turned away other qualified candidates without considering them for vacancies, or recruited in such a manner as to discourage white males from applying. When such allegations are submitted, and in the event a review of the facts substantiates discrimination against male and nonminority candidates or potential candidates in any particular case, we regard the practice as a violation of the executive order, in the same way that it would violate the executive order if an institution sanctioned a practice which discriminated against women and minorities.

However, our experience to date does not support the notion that such distortions are a universal, permanent, and growing phenomenon. Indeed, as our inquiries proceed, they are likely to counteract any further momentum in this direction. Presumably, universities, like other institutions of American life, do not operate in a vacuum; they learn from each other. And as HEW and the institutions with which it deals become better educated in the ways and means of carrying out an effective and legally sound affirmative action program, it is to be hoped that instances of what is commonly termed "reverse discrimination" will recede and ultimately vanish from the scene.

In light of these cases, it may be argued that some university officials have had difficulty grasping the salient points of permissable and impermissable forms of affirmative action. The "Guidelines" were issued to assist universities in this regard, although admittedly it appears in retrospect that a considerable amount of confusion prevailed prior to their issuance and that the Office for Civil Rights might have more vigorously attempted to set the record straight, even though numerous statements were released in the media to clarify points at issue.

For whatever reason, however, it is clear that some institutions chose the easy way out and elected to increase the number of minority and female employees illegally by the fastest route possible, apparently on the assumption that HEW was only interested in a numbers game and that the rules of the game didn't count. Segments of the intellectual community, depicted as beleaguered under the onslaught of HEW pressure, evidently yielded to a vague sense of affirmative action not in legitimate, non-discriminatory ways calculated to preserve the values of which Professors Hook and Bunzel speak so eloquently, but rather by naively applying precisely those tactics deplored by spokesmen and condemned by the executive order as unacceptable.

Running like a thread through the popular literature is the notion that such tactics were "necessary" in order to satisfy HEW, which is to impute to a highly well-educated sector of the population an astounding potential for capitulation to ill-founded principles which we are told would deal a heavy blow to their profession. When Professor Hook claimed that federal financial support would dry up unless "within a certain period of time, the proportion of members of minorities on the teaching and research staffs of universities approximate their proportion in the general population" (*The New York Times,* November 5, 1971, p. 39), he was mirroring and helping to perpetuate a rather primitive myth. In reality, HEW had never proposed that the racial and sex composition of faculties should reflect the general population. Nor had the government warned that the absence of a numerical increase in women and minority faculty members would alone and inexorably lead to the loss of federal financial support.

What this and similar articles had in common was a tendency to focus narrowly on the numbers aspect of affirmative action. HEW was pictured as pressing institutions not to correct practices that had led to underutilization of women and minorities, but to hire them—period. Admittedly, there may well have been instances, particularly prior to release of the clarifying "Guidelines," where HEW representatives, in communicating with individual institutions, unfortunately reinforced apprehensions by overstating their authority and the numerical aspect of the affirmative action obligation. Preoccupation with the end product of what is demonstrably an intricate and comprehensive exercise in institutional reform tended to oversimplify the issues and to highlight the perceived threat.

With respect to goals and timetables, their purpose is to overcome deficiencies in the utilization of minorities and women within a reasonable period of time. "Underutilization" is defined as having fewer minorities or women in a particular job classification than would reasonably be expected by their availability in the market or recruitment area. "Job classification" is defined as one or a group of jobs having similar content, wage rates, and opportunities.

The development of goals and timetables is but one integral part of an acceptable affirmative action plan. Specifically in this regard, the process whereby goals and timetables evolve and are implemented is crucial. For, if the institution gathers and properly evaluates all relevant data, carries out a thorough utilization analysis, secures accurate information on availability, and set in motion an internally well-understood recruitment program effectively designed to reach qualified women and minority candidates, this total process should lead to successful affirmative action in hiring policy. There is no intrinsic magic to figures. They are meaningful as targets and yardsticks only to the extent that a contractor, through a careful process of self-analysis and planning, gives them credibility. The process itself should act as a guarantee that the goals and timetables emerging as a consequence can realistically be met, precluding conditions under which they might be transformed into arbitrary or discriminatory devices.

enhancing the values of the university

In summary, certain conclusions may be drawn as to aspects of the early public debate on affirmative action and the extent to which the issues raised and discussed were an accurate reflection of the obligation and of efforts to enforce that obligation.

Some representatives of the academic community, reacting to the first tangible signs of enforcement, pictured the affirmative action obligation in overly-simplistic terms that served conveniently to underscore the perceived threat to academic standards. Implicitly, if not directly, the Department of Health, Education, and Welfare was accused of distorting affirmative action by requiring or condoning discriminatory practices, a proposition which we believe the record does not support.

Cases in which HEW required concrete commitments to develop data or correct deficiencies were not viewed as lawful attempts to enforce an obligation that would otherwise remain toothless, but as threats to cut off funds and as harassment.

This paper argues that affirmative action must be viewed as a process which, when faithfully executed, should serve to equalize opportunity without eroding valid and sound employment standards. Indeed, it is precisely because employment decisions have been based in part on practices and procedures that were unsound and invalid, to the disadvantage of certain persons or classes of persons, that federal contractors are now required to take affirmative measures. If, as most members of the academic community admit, past recruitment practices have tended to exclude or limit employment opportunities for qualified women and minorities, it is not far-fetched to conclude that colleges and universities may also have suffered losses. Curiously, in the articles cited, affirmative action is rarely conceptualized as having positive spin-off effects, in the sense that a university should benefit from seeking out new sources of talent and widening the applicant pool. Affirmative action challenges a university in ways that should enhance, rather than detract from, its value as a place of learning.

Peter E. Holmes was appointed director of the Office for Civil Rights in the Department of Health, Education, and Welfare in 1973. A 1961 graduate in political science from Northwestern University, he worked for Senators Frank J. Laushe of Ohio and Robert P. Griffin of Michigan before joining the Office for Civil Rights in 1969.

Examples of the impact of affirmative action on one institution have implications for planners and decision-makers at other colleges and universities.

implications for institutions

robert l. johnson

Genuine commitment to affirmative action permeates an institution, influencing all activities at all levels. It *changes* an institution. The nature of this change is in some ways obvious, but often subtle. If the change itself is difficult to quantify and analyze, its causes and costs are even more so. The change does not stem solely from federal requirements. Institutions of higher education are changing with the times, and federal legislation simply speeds the process and confirms our own sense of what is right and what must be done.

The first section of this chapter outlines some of the recent achievements in affirmative action at the University of California. It may provide useful comparative data for other institutions to assess their own progress on affirmative action. The second section describes a variety of additional activities and concerns at the university, which together indicate the potential impact of acting affirmatively to extend opportunities to women and minorities while retaining and strengthening standards of scholarship and excellence. The third section indicates some of the monetary costs of affirmative action to institutions of higher education.

Faculty recruitment in the University of California furnishes a particularly good example of achievement. Departments which would never have considered advertising faculty vacancies in journals read widely by women and minorities now do this routinely, with significant results.

On the Berkeley campus, for example, women represented 3 percent of the appointments to ladder rank faculty positions in 1967 and 6 percent in 1970; in 1973 women filled thirteen of the forty-eight vacancies, or 27 percent, at the assistant professor level where all but a few of the total vacancies occurred. A comparison of actual ladder rank appointments of women and minorities in 1972 with the expected numbers of such appointments, based on availability data, shows that the actual number of minorities hired was more than three times the expected number (eleven versus three). Women and minorities represented twenty-seven of the seventy-three new ladder rank appointments in that year, or 37 percent.

At the Santa Cruz campus, affirmative action goals for academic appointments in the fall of 1974 were set at eleven appointments for women and six for minorities. Of the thirty-five new fall appointees on that campus, four are minority women, ten are caucasian women and six are minority men, for a total of twenty appointees who are women or minorities or both. Thus the campus exceeded its goals for both minorities and women. At the San Diego campus, 39 percent of the 173 new fulltime faculty appointments from 1971 to 1973 were women and minorities.

There is also evidence of progress in the staff area. For example, minorities comprise 24.7 percent of the civilian labor force in the San Francisco-Oakland Standard Metropolitan Statistical Area. Currently, minorities comprise roughly 30 to 35 percent of all staff employees at the UC Berkeley campus, the San Francisco campus, and the Office of the President. These figures demonstrate that progress has been made in bringing minority group members into University employment. However, we are well aware that there are too few minorities and women in the higher paying professional and management job categories.

In the student area, substantial gains have been made in recruiting the ethnic minority student. The Educational Opportunity

Program (EOP), an undergraduate program to encourage disadvantaged youths to enroll in the university, had an enrollment in 1965-1966 of one hundred students on six campuses. By 1972-1973, 7679 students on eight campuses were participating in the program. In 1972-1973, ethnic minority students made up 83 percent of the students participating in the EOP program. I would emphasize that the university has put $30 million of its own resources into that program between 1967 and 1972. Since 1968, there has also been a substantial increase in applications and enrollment in the graduate financial assistance programs for ethnic minority students organized at the Berkeley, Davis, and Los Angeles campuses.

Policies governing university employees have been altered remarkably. Maternity leave benefits have been implemented, nepotism policies essentially gutted, and retirement policies revised. As evidence of a commitment beyond that required by law, the university has implemented two programs—the Affirmative Action Construction Program and the Minority Vendor Program—which show remarkable potential to extend affirmative action principles to the business arena. And now we are launching a comprehensive, universitywide student affirmative action effort.

I can say with conviction that we are a better institution for all this. Although the cost has been heavy, the benefits are certain.

opportunities to act affirmatively

Among the variety of additional activities and concerns which together indicate the impact of affirmative action on institutions of higher education are the following.

Employee Training. To some extent, this effort can be translated into dollars. But, insofar as mobility of women and minorities within the university's workforce depends on supervisors who are trained to upgrade and encourage employees and who can take time away from general administrative duties for this, the cost of training cannot be assessed.

On the staff side, training emphasis has been on the education of supervisors to an understanding of affirmative action as it related to employment interviews, selection among candidates, performance evaluation, and identification of employees for promotion. Two programs intended to develop meaningful support for the university's affirmative action programs were developed last year at the universitywide level in coordination with the campus training officers: Performance Appraisal and Supervisor-Supervisee Training.

Employee training and development programs vary in availability and sophistication from campus to campus. Each campus does maintain training programs, however, and is expanding those programs with emphasis on affirmative action principles. Courses are offered to employees, without cost and during working hours, on subjects ranging from shorthand to a program for women entitled "How to Stop Discriminating Against Yourself." University training efforts include a personnel policy which permits employees to draw up an employee development plan and, based on this, take courses at a variety of educational institutions with reimbursement for fees from the university.

On the academic side, a special summer benefits package is proposed for faculty at a cost of $2000 per participant. This would enable junior faculty to be given this sum for purposes such as summer research salary, computer time, travel to libraries, and laboratory assistance. This program would help in enabling new women and minority faculty members, most of whom have heavy teaching and student counseling assignments, to complete the research necessary for advancement.

Related Programs. Two programs discussed here reflect the university's commitment to affirmative action in the broadest sense. One of these, the Minority Vendor Program, was designed to increase the university's purchasing volume conducted with minority-owned and operated businesses. In a four-year period, this volume has risen from virtually zero to over $1.5 million after a strenuous effort on the part of material managers. With existing staff, we anticipate doubling that figure next year. No subsidy of minority business is involved; materials are obtained only on a low-bid basis. Costs of the program relate to identification of minority vendors, matching vendor abilities to university needs, training vendors in the processes of university bidding, encouraging submission of bids and shepherding paper work, and education of university staff to the importance of this effort. We had estimated a cost of $142,000 for this program in the current year. Although it now appears that no university funds will be available, funds may be available from the State Minority Business Agency.

The second program, Affirmative Action Construction Program, we believe to be one of the most comprehensive of its type in the country. Designed to prevent discrimination on university construction jobs and provide positions for members of minority groups at every level of the trade, the program will enable the university to provide leadership in setting a trend for the requirement of affirmative action programs on all construction jobs.

Briefly, the program consists of two major components: the education of all contractors and subcontractors to federal and university affirmative action requirements, and the provision of assistance to such contractors in developing affirmative action programs; and the determination of bidder eligibility under affirmative action program requirements and the monitoring of all construction jobs to ensure strict compliance with affirmative action programs and principles.

Much of the work of this program is handled at the campus level by existing staff. In addition, $80,000 will be expended at the universitywide level to conduct the educational programs, develop appropriate personnel goals, and monitor contract compliance.

Student Programs. While there are presently no federal regulations requiring the development and implementation of student affirmative action programs, the University of California has moved ahead in this area. Our commitment to action on student enrollment stems from our belief that institutions of higher education have a fundamental obligation to assist in enlarging the pool of women and members of minority groups qualified to hold professional positions. We also believe that affirmative actions are necessary to comply with the spirit of Title VI of the Civil Rights Act, as well as Title IX of the Education Amendments.

Since 1965 the university has been engaged in an educational opportunity program designed to provide access to the university and academic support services for undergraduate students who, for socioeconomic reasons, might not otherwise have pursued higher education; to increase the number of students from the ethnic and economic groups underrepresented in the university; and to increase the cultural diversity of the university's student enrollment. In 1965-1966, there were one hundred students enrolled in the program on six campuses. By 1972-1973, 7679 students were participating in the program on eight campuses, and the annual budget had grown to $13,887,000 including $1,759,000 in administrative costs which include 134 full-time employees.

Various support services are provided by the campuses for the EOP student, including initial recruitment, preadmission counseling, and ongoing academic and personal counseling once enrolled. Tutorial services are available. Financial assistance is also available to the EOP student. Of the 7679 EOP students registered for academic year 1972-1973, 84 percent received some form of financial aid. Of the financial aid funds available to EOP students, 44 percent was funded from federal sources and 56 percent from university resources.

Campuses have also recognized the need for special services for the low-income, disadvantaged, or ethnic minority graduate student. One campus has an organized recruiting committee whose purpose is "to search for the student who would not otherwise enroll in graduate study without special recruitment, financial assistance, and/or academic support services." For the most part, recruiting efforts and academic support services have been left to the discretion and resources of individual departments and professional schools at each of the campuses. Faculty and students donate an appreciable amount of their own time for recruitment. Many third and fourth grade graduate students provide tutorial support for the first year graduate student. These efforts are reflected in the dramatic increase, over 500 percent, in the number of applications to the graduate financial assistance programs, and the fact that an appreciable number of the students participating in these programs are obtaining graduate degrees. The social sciences and the professional schools have made the greatest advancement toward recruiting and graduating the ethnic minority student.

Recently, interested parties from the campuses have convened to discuss ways of combining campus efforts to attract more ethnic minority students, particularly to the hard sciences. This group has suggested publication of a booklet describing the various programs and financial aid available on each of the campuses for disadvantaged or ethnic minority graduate students (or both). They have also proposed an active admissions and financial aid referral system and a uniform "offer" date for financial aid. The group plans to serve as an information exchange and to use their combined interests and knowledge to find financial and institutional support for recruitment, tutorial, counseling, and financial aid services for these students.

Given the substantial progress in these specific student programs, the university is, nonetheless, now in the process of reviewing all aspects of the educational process—including recruitment, admissions, academic and student life support, and financial aids—in an effort to identify any barriers to equal opportunity. Once such barriers are identified, we must move aggressively to eliminate them through policy changes and corrective programs.

costs of affirmative action

The U.S. Department of Health, Education, and Welfare has made it clear that the affirmative action plan negotiated between Berkeley and HEW will serve as a model for all other affirmative action plans negotiated between institutions of higher education and HEW. Monetary costs imposed on the University of California for affirmative action might also be imposed on all other institutions, if the current plan does, in fact, become a model for all other institutions.

Much of the cost of our affirmative action efforts, probably a majority of the cost, can never be calculated, though real dollars are involved. So far as we can calculate cost, we estimate it to have been more than $2 million in 1973-1974, of which $350,000 was new money—$250,000 appropriated by the State of California, and $100,000 appropriated by the Regents of the University. For 1974-1975, the state has continued the $250,000 appropriation; the Regents' appropriation is $500,000; we will spend over $2 million by absorbing costs within regular institutional resources; and another $500,000 from internal funds is specifically earmarked for affirmative action—for a total of approximately $3 million.

Funds specifically allocated for affirmative action in 1974-1975 and costs absorbed internally relate to five broad categories of expense: program coordination and administration ($385,000 earmarked), employment recruiting $237,000 earmarked), training (no specific appropriation), data production and analysis (no specific appropriation), and related programs ($128,000 earmarked, including $40,000 for student affirmative action). Consider the costs in two of these five areas.

Employment Recruiting. The university has been engaged in a vigorous effort to search out, identify, and encourage applicants from groups underrepresented in our workforce—with special emphasis on those occupational categories where women and minorities are underrepresented. This includes contact with national and local organizations, community groups, and a variety of recruiting sources. On some campuses, recruiters are assigned full-time to this outreach recruiting effort. Extensive advertising costs are incurred in conformity with the requirement for a full-scale search and recruitment of a diversified pool of candidates. Additional costs are incurred in paying travel expenses of candidates brought for interview.

On the academic side, for instance, departments have normally reimbursed travel expenses of only one or two candidates. Financial restrictions have meant that only candidates who fit a previously conceived image of "best bet" have been invited. Since women and minority scholars often may not fit this stereotypic image, they may have been less likely to be invited for interviews. Faculty members are aware of this problem and are most anxious to correct it by seeking to ensure that an honest and vigorous search be made for all competitive candidates. We estimate an additional expense of $1000 per new ladder rank appointment to permit a much-needed expansion of the interview process, totaling perhaps as much as $620,000 in a year.

On the staff side, costs of advertising, long distance calls, and travel expenses recently exceeded $3000 for each of two high-level management positions. Over five hundred applications were received for one of these openings, executive director of computing, and each application received close attention. The $3000-plus price tag for recruiting does not, of course, include the time of members of the search committee to scrutinize resumes and interview candidates.

Data Production and Analysis. Generation and analysis of data includes the high cost of adapting our computer information systems to the demands of affirmative action reporting requirements. This has been expensive and complicated, and the process is by no means complete. Further technical improvements are necessary so that our data processing system will be modified to provide comparative studies based on historical personnel information.

We must produce reports on university workforce composition by sex, ethnic group, and occupational category and must maintain detailed records of all internal personnel actions. This involves not only the expense of computer hardware and software, keypunch operators, programers, machine time, and report production, but also the cost of personnel throughout the university system who develop and maintain manual records and who analyze these and computer printouts to produce a variety of statistical reports.

It is in this area, particularly, that the costly effects of changing federal definitions and inconsistent requirements are felt. Seemingly minor differences in reporting requirements, such as counting or not counting noncitizens separately, or including or excluding other nonwhites from the total minority category, necessitate reprograming and recalculating all down the line.

One very costly area which we have only begun to explore concerns the in-depth analyses of individual personnel actions which must occur, under Executive Order 11246 and implementing regulations, when data indicate a disparate effect on women or minorities. Such analyses may involve an individual-by-individual review of all job applicants within a particular occupational category, and a comparison of their qualifications with qualifications listed for vacancies and the qualifications of candidates who were appointed. An in-depth analysis now being conducted on the Berkeley campus involves a review of the qualifications and appointment levels of all new ladder rank faculty in a three-year period. Should this review indicate genuine salary inequities, compensatory payments will be needed. Nowhere in the budget figures I quoted earlier is this taken into account, nor can we guess what the cost, if any, might be.

Quite apart from federal reporting requirements, however, the expense involved in data gathering and analysis relates directly to the monitoring process and the identification of possible problems. Only by learning where these problems exist can we investigate them and take corrective steps. So we are committed to the expense involved, major as this is.

Robert L. Johnson was vice president for student affairs at the University of Kentucky before becoming vice chancellor for student affairs at Berkeley in 1968. He served as vice chancellor for administration at Berkeley and then as vice president for administration of the entire University of California before assuming the vice presidency for university relations in 1972. Besides being responsible for university relations, student affairs, and financial aids, he is the affirmative action officer for the Office of the President, co-chairman of the Chicano Task Force, and holder of an academic appointment in Berkeley's School of Public Health.

The president of the University of Michigan suggests changes in federal policies and, disagreeing with Sandler and Holmes, advocates private arbitration.

implications for government

robben w. fleming

This chapter deals with the issue of eligibility conditions the federal government imposes on the receipt of federal funds by an institution and the policies and procedures used in enforcing those conditions. That issue is controversial, sensitive, and characterized by a good deal more heat than light.

principles vs. procedures

Though there are some people who will deny it, most observers will concede that both race and sex discrimination have occurred in colleges and universities. This being so, it is not surprising that federal laws were passed which outlawed discrimination. These laws covered a wide range of activities, including student admissions, financial aid, employment and pay practices, and sports activities. Penalties for noncompliance included loss of eligibility for federal funds, affirmative action for remedial purposes, and back pay for past infractions.

Effective law enforcement is in large measure a function of the acceptability of the law in question. Since laws which attempt to change deeply rooted social views cannot help but be controversial, any federal agency which is faced with the enforcement problem has an unenviable task. Thus those of us who are critical have an obligation to state our views in a constructive manner. I am critical; therefore I shall try also to be constructive.

I agree with the social objectives of legislation which tries to wipe out discrimination based upon race, sex, and ethnic origin. My criticism of government programs designed to accomplish this objective is threefold. In the first place, the programs tend to be overly bureaucratic and are therefore burdened with administrative procedures which are nearly impossible to successfully administer. Second, multiple and overlapping lines of jurisdiction among the courts, federal and state agencies, and attempted private grievance systems confuse those who believe they have been wronged and harass university administrators. Third, enforcement agencies tend to treat colleges and universities as though they were industrial plants, or at the very least identical within their own ranks, both of which are far from the truth.

problems of administration

The first criticism, that government agencies are overly bureaucratic, is illustrated by what the universities perceive to be an excessive demand for the production of documentary materials, plus due process deficiencies in allowing an appropriate hearing or appeal on the university's side of the case. In many cases the documents which are required are not in existence, particularly with respect to past practice. It is enormously costly to manually prepare such materials, although if the demand were prospective rather than retroactive much of it could be put on computers and be made more readily available. The relevance of some of the material is not evident; the cost of compiling the information is astonishing, particularly in view of the precarious financial position of most colleges and universities today.

On the due process front, universities are particularly disturbed by the way in which these matters are handled. Agency procedures and actions are inconsistent from one geographical area to another; attempts are made to withhold contracts before a fair hearing is accorded the institution; there are problems relating to the appeal process from regional offices; unreasonable time limits for response to agency interrogatories occur; and there are dubious standards of proof in establishing the existence of discrimination.

It appears to many of us that steps could be taken to remedy these deficiencies if the agencies were to provide better training for their field and regional staffs; if there were manuals providing for uniform standards and activities in the regional offices; if there were a policy of giving early notice to institutions of the status of their affirmative action plans and of impending compliance reviews; if there were written procedures guaranteeing institutions full and fair hearings before contracts are withheld; and if there were the right, not just a privilege granted at agency discretion, to appeal actions by regional offices.

The cost and administrative burden of compiling information naturally evokes little sympathy from those who feel that they have been discriminated against. Indeed, the cost and effort might be justified if it could be demonstrated that it is productive. On the contrary, it is evident that enforcement agencies are not staffed to examine and analyze the mountains of material which they are accumulating. Unless the whole procedure is a form of punishment which is designed to produce better conduct in the future, it is hard to see what really useful purpose it is serving. Meanwhile, it is imposing an enormous burden on universities. Surely a far simpler system could be devised which would be at least as effective, and I am confident that the academic associations would join in a cooperative effort to devise such a system.

conflicts of jurisdiction

A second, and in some ways even more aggravating problem, is the multiple jurisdiction monstrosity which has been created. This confusing hodgepodge gives a wide variety of agencies power to move into the same or similar areas. The Department of Health, Education, and Welfare; the Department of Labor; the Equal Opportunity Commission; the courts; and a series of state agencies all fish in the same general pond. Nevertheless, published figures show enormous case backlogs which cannot reasonably be expected to be handled.

Out of a long personal experience in private arbitration in the labor-management field, I would argue that there is a relatively easy way to cope with this problem. In the labor area, courts and administrative agencies honor arbitration pacts which operate fairly and within the framework of the law. If this rule prevailed in the area of discrimination, as it presently does not, there would be an incentive to universities to establish such private tribunals on an impartial basis. There would be a similar incentive to the grievant to utilize the system because it could be made quick and effective. As things now stand, the grievant naturally wishes to have his cake and eat it too by having multiple forums, and there is no incentive to a university to provide an impartial system at some cost to itself when there is no assurance that its ruling will be final.

We have done some experimenting with a similar, though not identical, tribunal system at the University of Michigan. Overall it has worked reasonably well, but it is now falling apart because impartial tribunal members do not want to waste their time serving on a body which has no capacity to make a binding decision and because grievants who appear before it do not wish to forego their further opportunities before other agencies.

Should the idea of private, impartial, binding tribunals be appealing, we should consider requiring administrative agencies and courts to respect such decisions providing they were fairly conducted and within the law. I am confident that an effective system could be devised with some speed.

denial of diversity

Finally, government agencies which have gained their principal experience with discrimination on the industrial scene tend to treat colleges and universities as though they were factories, or at the very least identical within their own ranks. This is understandable since this is where most enforcement personnel seem to have had their experience and because their task is so overwhelming that they see no way of coping with it except in the most simplistic terms. The academic community is, of course, enormously diverse and differs from an industrial operation.

From the university standpoint, the most sensitive aspect of this last problem is in the hiring of faculty. It is clearly in the best interests of the country to have universities hire as faculty members the most competent people they can find. Insofar as they have failed to do so in the past for reasons of discrimination such practices should be abolished. The danger, however, is that the absence of discrimination will be judged solely on the basis of the statistical representation of individuals by sex, race, and ethnic origin. It would not, in my view, be unfair to impose upon universities the burden of demonstrating when challenged that their choice of faculty members is based on a fair search for candidates and on the absence of any kind of discrimination. To impose a statistical measure of success or failure is, I think, both unworkable and counterproductive. Unfortunately, it is not clear where the federal agencies or the courts are headed in this respect.

Though I do not purport to speak for anyone but myself, I believe that my criticisms are widely shared by other presidents of universities. Certainly they are the criticisms which I hear in the course of our meetings. I am critical of the system employed, not the individuals who seek to make it operate. The system imposes undue data collection responsibilities on the universities, and the data when submitted give rise to analytical problems which are beyond the time and energy capability of the agency. The web of interrelated enforcement responsibilities is confusing to all, enormously overburdened, incapable of coping with its backlog of cases, and susceptible to replacement by a far more efficient and expeditious system. The practice of treating colleges and universities as though they were business firms ignores longstanding differences and practices which have contributed to the growth and development of a strong system of higher education in this country.

punishment or incentives?

It would appear that the enforcement program on conditions of university eligibility for federal funds is based upon a principle of punishment. I would argue that it would be more effective if it were based on a system of incentives. I do not see the university world fighting to preserve discrimination. Few if any segments of society are more likely to be favorable to change in social practice. It is possible for the government and the universities to work together in this respect. An indication from the Congress that it would welcome a new and more effective way of insuring compliance with its eligibility principles would, I am sure, be welcomed in the university community.

Robben W. Fleming has been president of the University of Michigan since 1968. Previously he served as director of the Institute of Industrial and Labor Relations and professor of law at the University of Illinois and chancellor of the University of Wisconsin. An industrial arbitrator, he has been president of the National Academy of Arbitrators and has assisted the Federal Mediation and Conciliation Service and the American Arbitration Association.

Data on sex and ethnic differences in academic achievement document a pervasive climate of different expectations about behavior on the basis of sex and ethnicity and indicate the need for affirmative action at five critical points in the academic system.

critical points for affirmative action

lucy w. sells

Effective affirmative action at faculty hiring levels, as required by federal policy, rests ultimately on increasing availability pools of women and minorities at each of five critical points in the educational structure where career decisions are made: (1) enrollment in high school mathematics, (2) application for graduate school, (3) survival in doctoral programs, (4) faculty recruitment and hiring, and (5) faculty promotion and tenure. Data to support the importance of these five filtering points come from a variety of sources.

high school mathematics

The first filtering point is adequate high school mathematics preparation in order to keep students' choice of undergraduate major open. There is considerable variation in the amount of mathe-

This chapter is based on part on data gathered by the Carnegie Commission on Higher Education from its National Survey of Higher Education with support from the United States Office of Education.

matics required for admission to college by type of institution, whether research university, state college, community college, or private college, but some majors at all institutions are effectively closed to students if they fail to take enough mathematics in high school.

The University of California is a good example of a research oriented public university where policies operate to filter women and minorities out of certain majors. Its data can be extended to many other institutions as well. The university requires the equivalent of two years of high school mathematics for freshman admission to any of the nine campuses. It further specifies three and a half years of mathematics in high school as the prerequisite for the standard freshman calculus course—a course required for majoring in chemistry, engineering, some agricultural sciences, some business administration, all of the hard sciences, most of the biological sciences, and the advanced quantitative methods required in doctoral programs in the social sciences. Until very recently, there was no formalized mechanism for students entering Berkeley to overcome deficiencies in this prerequisite.

To test the contention that inadequate mathematics preparation in high school presents a serious constraint on women's choice of undergraduate major in college, I hypothesized that women applying for admission at Berkeley would be less likely to have taken advanced mathematics than men. (It was not possible to code by ethnicity because state law forbids the collection of data on ethnicity on applications for admission lest it be used to discriminate against ethnic minorities.) A systematic sample of transcripts from the applicants for admission as freshmen at Berkeley for the fall of 1972 revealed that while 57 percent of the men had prepared themselves for the standard calculus course by taking the three and a half units of mathematics, only 8 percent of the women had done so. The difference of forty-nine percentage points is evidence both of dramatic differences in the ambitions and aspirations of young men and women and important sociological differences in expectations for them by individuals who are significant in their lives: parents, peers, teachers, and counselors.

To test the hypothesis of differing climates of expectations and social support leading to decisions to take mathematics in high school, members of an upper division social science class completed a questionnaire about performance in elementary school arithmetic and in high school mathematics; expectations and encouragement by teachers, parents, and peers; extent of high school mathematics training beyond the minimal two unit requirement; and an open-ended question, "What do you consider to be the most important factor which influenced your interest and aptitude for doing mathematics?" A strong relationship was obvious between presence or absence of encouragement and whether or not students took mathematics beyond the minimal requirement for admission to the University of California. (Q = 0.94, statistically significant at the 0.01 level.) A strong relationship also appeared between having social support for mathematics and performing well in the advanced mathematics courses. These data point to the need for experimental projects designed to increase the level of social encouragement for undertaking advanced high school mathematics, independent of sex or ethnicity. In this connection, a dramatic increase occurred between 1972 and 1973 at Berkeley in the percentage of freshmen women taking the high school prerequisite to the standard calculus course; from 8 percent to 32 percent, while the percentage of men preparing for the course rose from 57 percent to 65 percent. It appears that the high school counselors are doing a more effective job in helping all students keep their options open as far as free choice of undergraduate major is concerned.

Table 1 shows how the high school mathematics filter operates to keep women out of university majors which require calculus in their curriculum. The only two exceptions to this pattern among the 15 schools listed are in agricultural sciences, where 88 percent of the students in nutritional science are women despite intensive mathematics and chemistry requirements, and in law, which has a low proportion of women and no mathematics requirement. In both cases, it appears that traditional sex role stereotyping about "appropriate" careers for men and women are operating in choice of field. Otherwise, the more mathematics required in an undergraduate curriculum, the lower the proportion of women enrolled—whether one looks at schools and colleges or at the four fields within letters and science (humanities, social sciences, biological sciences, and physical sciences) or at individual majors within fields.

It should be pointed out that aggregation of departments within fields conceals sharp variation among those departments. When a high requirement of mathematics is in the curriculum, the result is a low percentage of undergraduate women majoring in the

Table 1. University of California, Berkeley: Percentage of Women at Undergraduate and Graduate Levels by Schools and Colleges Controlling for Mathematics Requirement in the major

	Percentage of Women		*Total Number of Students*	
School or College	*Under-graduate*	*Graduate*	*Under-graduate*	*Graduate*
Mathematics Required				
Agricultural Sciences (including Nutritional Science)	48	30	651	242
Chemistry	14	9	358	394
Engineering	3	2	1361	1336
Environmental Design	17	25	748	424
Business Administration	17	9	693	565
Forestry and Conservation	7	6	132	89
Optometry	17	12	121	112
Letters and Science:				
Biological Sciences	33	29	1085	465
Physical Sciences	22	11	664	817
Total	20	12	5813	4444
Mathematics Not Required				
Criminology	46	38	201	57
Education	NP	54	NP	953
Journalism	NP	50	NP	42
Law	NP	25	NP	851
Librarianship	NP	66	NP	205
Social Welfare	NP	59	NP	245
Ethnic Studies	55	NP	33	
Letters and Science				
Humanities	58	48	2001	965
Social Sciences	46	33	3754	1082
Total	50	41	5989	4400
Mathematics Difference	30*	29*		

Source: University of California, Berkeley, *Campus Statistics, Fall 1972* and *Year 1971-1972*, Table 6, pages 22-25.

NP = No program at this level.
*Percentage difference is statistically significant at the 0.05 level, using a conservative estimate of a two-tailed test.

department. This relationship is even stronger among majors in the humanities and social sciences than it is between these broad fields and the physical sciences. For example, while Table 1 shows that 58 percent of the undergraduates in the humanities are women, compared with 22 percent in the physical sciences (for a difference of 36 percent) within the humanities, 83 percent of the undergraduates in history of art (which requires no calculus) are women, compared with 24 percent of the undergraduates in philosophy (which requires logic)—a difference of 59 percent. In the social sciences, the within field difference is 47 percent: 61 percent of the anthropology majors are women, compared to 14 percent in economics, which requires completion of the high school trigonometry sequence. These within field differences point up the dangers inherent in aggregating fields for estimating availability pools and for measuring underutilization at the faculty hiring level.

The patterns of choice of undergraduate major among ethnic minorities is similar to those of women students, except that Asian minorities are over-represented in the mathematics based fields. Table 2 shows the percentage of letters and science students majoring in the physical sciences, life sciences, or mathematics, by sex and ethnicity. There is a strong interaction between sex, ethnicity, and choice of these three fields. While 68 percent of the Asian men are enrolled in these curricula, only 17 percent of nonminority women and 17 percent of all other minority women are majoring in them. Conversely, the percentage of Asian women in these fields slightly exceeds that of nonminority men and other minority men. I attribute these very large sex and ethnic differences to cultural factors rather than to genetic factors.

Table 2. Percentage Majoring in Physical Sciences, Life Sciences, and Mathematics by Sex and Ethnicity

	Percentage			*Total Number*	
	Men	*Women*	*Sex Difference*	*Men*	*Women*
Asian	68	45	23*	615	538
All Other Minority	37	17	20*	697	412
Nonminority	41	17	24*	4094	3040
Total	44	21	23*	5406	3990

Source: University of California, Berkeley, Student Resource Survey, Spring 1972.

*Percentage difference is statistically significant at the 0.05 level, using a conservative estimate of a two-tailed test.

application to graduate school

The second filtering point in educational achievement for women and minorities is the decision to apply for graduate study. Table 3 shows the dropoff in the percentage of women in undergraduate and graduate study at Berkeley. This dropoff directly affects the availability of women for recruitment and hiring at the faculty level. Thus, while 22 percent of the undergraduates in the physical sciences are women, only 11 percent of the graduate students are women. A similar pattern exists in the reduction of Asian and other minority students from undergraduate to graduate study.

Table 3. Dropoff in Percentage Women from Undergraduate to Graduate Level

	Undergraduate	*Graduate*	*Dropoff*	*Dropoff Rate***
Mathematics Required				
Agricultural Sciences	48	30	–18*	–0.38
Chemistry	14	9	– 5	–0.36
Engineering	3	2	– 1	–0.33
Environmental Design	17	25	+ 8*	+0.47
Business Administration	17	9	– 8*	–0.47
Forestry and Conservation	7	6	– 1	–0.14
Optometry	17	12	– 5	–0.29
Letters and Science				
Biological Sciences	33	29	– 4	–0.12
Physical Sciences	22	11	–11*	–0.50
Total	20	12	– 8*	–0.40
Mathematics Not Required				
Criminology	46	38	– 8	–0.17
Letters and Science				
Humanities	58	48	–10*	–0.17
Social Sciences	46	33	–13*	–0.28
Total	50	40	–10*	–0.20

Source: Calculated from data in Table 1.

*Percentage dropoff from undergraduate to graduate level is statistically significant at the 0.05 level.

**Dropoff rate is calculated by the formula

$$\frac{\%\ \text{Undergraduates} - \%\ \text{Graduates}}{\%\ \text{Undergraduates}}$$

At the second filter it is clear from the data provided by the Berkeley Graduate Division that women and minorities are being admitted in the same proportion in which they apply. The problem is that they are not applying to graduate school in the same proportion as they earn undergraduate degrees in their respective schools, colleges, fields, and departments.

Recent data from Berkeley show large and statistically significant sex and ethnic differences in the percentage of students reporting the doctorate as the highest level of education they plan to complete. In the College of Letters and Science, 63 percent of the men compares to 36 percent of the women aspire to the doctorate. The fields in the college are reported in Table 4, with the humanities and social sciences grouped, and with physical sciences, life sciences, and mathematics as another group. In both groups, men

Table 4. Percentage of Doctoral Aspirants by Sex and Ethnicity, Controlling for Field

	Percentage of Doctoral Aspirants		*Sex*	*Total Number of Students*	
	Men	*Women*	*Difference*	*Men*	*Women*
	Humanities and Social Sciences				
Minority					
Asian American	44	21	23*	195	295
All Other Minority	59	34	25*	438	343
Nonminority	57	33	24*	2419	2511
Total	56	32	24*	3052	3149
	Physical Sciences, Life Sciences, and Mathematics				
Minority					
Asian American	65	32	33*	420	243
All Other Minority	72	62	10	259	69
Nonminority	75	58	17*	1675	529
Total	73	51	22*	2354	841
	Field Difference				
Minority					
Asian American	21*	11*			
All Other Minority	18*	25*			
Nonminority	13*	28*			

Source: University of California, Berkeley, Student Resource Survey, Spring, 1972.

*Percentage difference is statistically significant at the 0.05 level.

are more likely to plan on the doctorate than women, and non-Asians more likely to do so than Asians.

If we assume that talent and willingness to work are randomly distributed between the sexes and among ethnic groups, the data suggest both a differential climate of encouragement and support for application to graduate school and a differential climate of aspirations about one's career goals, based on sex and ethnicity. In most social systems based on meritocracy and achievement, aspirations to move up the ladder are very much shaped by those who have already demonstrated their achievement, independently of the standards of evaluation and criteria for achievement involved. In the academic system, this means that faculty have the power to encourage potential talent regardless of the sex or ethnicity of the person who displays that talent. The primary goal of affirmative action is to free all persons to develop their talents and energies to highest potential, regardless of sex or ethnicity. Faculty members should recognize that their values of scholarship and excellence will be enhanced through affirmative action by removing previous constraints on the development of talent.

graduate support

The third filter in educational achievement for women and minorities involves survival in doctoral programs. Because there are insufficient data available on minorities at this level, the remainder of this paper is based on data about women. However, it is clear that the causal mechanisms which operate to filter women out of the doctoral pool operate even more intensely against minorities. These mechanisms include a social climate which systematically lowers aspirations, expectations, sense of competence, and self-esteem, both actively by discouragement and passively by absence of support and encouragement.

The facts in this section come from a secondary analysis of data gathered on Woodrow Wilson Fellows who entered graduate school from 1958 through 1963 (Mooney, 1966). At the time of the study, 49 percent of the Woodrow Wilson Fellows had not yet earned the doctorate, and were no longer in graduate school. Among the men, 44 percent had dropped out, compared with 64 percent of the women. Table 5 shows both large sex differences and field differences in dropouts. Interestingly enough, however,

Table 5. Woodrow Wilson Fellows, 1958-1963
Dropouts by Sex and Discipline

	Percentage			*Total Number*	
	Men	*Women*	*Sex Difference*	*Men*	*Women*
Humanities	52	66	14*	1966	1192
Social Sciences	46	64	18*	2123	667
Physical Sciences	26	62	36*	1182	172
Biological Sciences	20	36	16*	112	69
All Disciplines	44	64	20*	5383	2100
Discipline Difference	32*	30*			

Source: The original Mooney data were obtained for secondary analysis by permission of Janet Mitchell, director of the Woodrow Wilson Dissertation Fellowship Program.

*Sex and discipline differences of dropouts are statistically significant at the 0.05 level.

women in the biological sciences were less likely to drop out than men in the humanities and social sciences. The contrast between the sexes in dropout rates between the physical sciences and the biological sciences—36 percent compared to 16 percent—suggests a more supportive climate for women in the biological sciences.

The effect of having second year financial support on dropout rates operates differently for men and for women. In the humanities, dropouts among men with no second year support are 57 percent, compared with 43 percent for those with second year support, a difference of 14 percent. For women with no second year support, 72 percent dropped out, compared with 43 percent of women with second year support, a difference of 29 percent. In the physical and biological sciences, the effect of second year support is even more dramatic for women. Dropout rates for men go from 33 percent to 16 percent, for a 17 percent decline, with second year support, compared with a reduction from 66 percent to 26 percent, or a 40 percent decline, for women.

This large difference reflects the special kind of self-esteem and assertiveness it presently takes for a woman to think her work is good enough to justify applying for support. If she thinks well of her work, she is free to communicate her worth to others. Traditional female socialization has taught young girls that assertiveness is unfeminine, just as traditional ethnic socialization had taught blacks that the Uncle Tom role was the key to their survival in a racist society.

After the first year of graduate school, department chairmen were asked to rate the Woodrow Wilson Fellows compared with other graduate students in their respective departments. Table 6 shows the effect on sex differences in dropouts when graduate rating by faculty is controlled. A reasonable assumption is that in a pure meritocracy, where talent and willingness to work are the primary determinants of success, dropout rates would be low among those rated *excellent* by their faculty, and high among those rated *average.* In fact, the overall sex difference in dropouts of 20 percent rises to 26 percent among those rated *excellent*. When field is also controlled, it rises to 38 percent in the physical sciences. The critical point is that there is no statistically significant difference in the dropout rates of women rated *excellent* and of men who are rated *average* by their faculty. This fact points to a second major goal of affirmative action—to make it possible for the achievements of women and minorities rated *excellent* to surpass those of white men rated *average.*

From 1962 to 1968 a dramatic reduction occurred in the fourth year dropout rates among women doctoral students at Berkeley. In the entering cohort of 1962, 22 percent of the 1093 men had dropped out of the doctoral program by the fourth year. In that same cohort, 42 percent of the women had dropped out by the fourth year. Six years later, the sex differences in fourth year dropout rates had disappeared for the 1968 cohorts. By 1972, 27 percent of the men had dropped out, compared to 27 percent of the women.

Reduction of attrition among women at Berkeley has been

Table 6. Woodrow Wilson Fellows, 1958-1963
Dropouts by Sex and Graduate Rating

	Percentage			*Total Number*	
Graduate Rating	*Men*	*Women*	*Sex Difference*	*Men*	*Women*
Excellent	32	58	26*	860	270
Very good	44	67	23*	677	271
Average	61	80	19*	455	175
Graduate Rating Difference	29*	22*			

Source: *Supra.*

*Sex and rating differences of dropouts are statistically significant at the 0.05 level.

most dramatic in the English and history departments. In the entering class of 1962, 88 percent of the women in English had dropped out by the fourth year, compared with 47 percent of the women in the class of 1968, a reduction of 41 percent. In the entering class of 1962, 81 percent of the women in history had dropped out by the fourth year, compared with 41 percent of the entering class of 1968, a reduction of 40 percent.

This reduction of attrition of women doctoral students has occurred independently of difficult efforts to achieve a meaningful affirmative action plan by the administration. It can be attributed both to the powerful social support of the women's movement, and to the fact that faculty at Berkeley are learning not to impose expectations and stereotypes based on the behavior of some women in the 1960s on the behavior of other women in the 1970s.

faculty recruitment

The fourth filtering point in educational achievement of women and minorities is the traditional academic recruiting system, sometimes called the "old boy" or "buddy" system. Until federal policy on affirmative action required open search and recruitment procedures, job openings at first rate doctoral institutions had often been limited to acquaintances and colleagues of those in a position to do the recruiting and hiring.

In 1968, the Carnegie Commission on Higher Education sponsored a national survey of higher education (Trow and others, 1972). Analysis of the data on faculty members at a sample of universities designated *high quality* shows very large sex and discipline differences in the percentage of affirmative responses to the question, "As a graduate student, was there a faculty member who acted as your sponsor when you were looking for your first job?" (See Table 7.) With the exception of the social sciences, in which there were no sex differences, the pattern of sex and discipline differences in sponsorship is consistent with the pattern of dropouts by sex and discipline in the Woodrow Wilson data. That is, smaller proportions of women received this kind of important support, and smaller proportions of people in the humanities received it than in the biological and physical sciences. The discipline difference is almost twice as large for women (27 percent) as it is for men (15 percent).

Table 7. Faculty at High Quality Universities Who Reported Having Had a Faculty Sponsor, by Sex and Field**

	Percentage			*Total Number*	
Field	*Men*	*Women*	*Sex Difference*	*Men*	*Women*
Humanities	56	41	15*	1719	235
Physical Sciences	66	45	21	1526	65
Social Sciences	71	68	3	1445	146
Biological Sciences	64	46	18*	1069	110
Total	64	50	14*	5759	556

Source: Secondary Analysis of Data Gathered by the National Survey of Higher Education, Sponsored by the Carnegie Commission on Higher Education.

*Statistically significant at the 0.05 level.
**The Carnegie Commission data based on institutions designated *high quality university* do not include medium or low quality universities, four year colleges, or junior colleges.

The pattern of sex and discipline differences in dropouts is repeated in the pattern of graduate student responses to the Carnegie Commission survey question, "Does the Professor with whom you have the most contact outside the classroom regard you primarily as: a colleague; an apprentice; an employee; a student; no contact outside the classroom." The discipline differences are larger than the sex differences, with 72 percent of the men in psychology reporting collegial or apprentice relations with their primary faculty contact, compared with 39 percent of the men in mathematics. Nevertheless, among the women in psychology, 53 percent reported collegial or apprentice relations with their primary faculty contact, compared with 22 percent of the women in mathematics.

promotion and tenure

The fifth filter in educational achievement for women, but probably not for minorities, is the underutilization of women who have pulled themselves into the availability pool for faculty hiring by virtue of having earned the doctorate. Table 8 shows the juxtaposition of availability pools and utilization for selected disciplines. The availability pools are defined here as the percentage of women earning the doctorate in the decade of the 1960s for each field. Utilization is defined here as the percentage of women among those persons with a doctorate on the faculties of high quality universities in the Carnegie survey. This gives a conservative estimate of underutilization, since the proportion of women earning doctorates is higher among the high ranking institutions than among other universities (Sells, 1973, pp. 15-20).

Underutilization is largest in the humanities, which has an availability pool of 18 percent of the doctorates granted in the 1960s to women, but where only 8 percent of the faculty members with doctorates are women, giving an underutilization rate of 10 percent. A detail of this underutilization not shown in the summary information of Table 8 is an availability pool of 24 percent for women with doctorates in English, and utilization of only 5 percent, resulting in 18 percent underutilization.

Not only is the available pool of qualified women being underutilized in the sample of high quality universities; it is also disproportionately distributed at the lower end of faculty ranks. Table 9 shows the percentage of women among the faculty with doctorates by rank and field. For each field, the percentage of women gets larger down the ranks from full professor to instructor or lecturer. There are large and statistically significant differences in all but the physical sciences, where the small size of the availability pool places an artificial ceiling on underutilization.

The difference in the percentage of women from full professor to instructor or lecturer grows *larger* with each increase in the length of time spent at the institution. Among those who have been at their institution up to three years, the rank difference is fourteen

Table 8. Women in Availability Pools and Women Ph.D.s on Faculties of High Quality Universities for Academic Disciplines

Discipline	*Availability Pool Percentage (Number)*	*Utilization Percentage (Number)*	*Under-utilization*
Humanities	18 (22,392)	8 (1525)	10*
Social Sciences	15 (22,854)	8 (1319)	7*
Biological Sciences	14 (17,708)	8 (957)	6*
Physical Sciences	5 (31,902)	3 (1388)	2
Total Academic	12 (94,856)	7 (5189)	5*

Source: *Availability Pools:* Women's Equity Action League, *Proportion of Doctorates Earned by Women, by Area and Field, 1960-1969,* June 1971. *Utilization:* Secondary Analysis of the National Survey of Higher Education, sponsored by the Carnegie Commission on Higher Education.

*Statistically significant at the 0.05 level.

Table 9. Women Among Faculty Members with Doctorates, by Rank and Field

	Full Professor Percentage (Number)	*Associate Professor Percentage (Number)*	*Assistant Professor Percentage (Number)*	*Instructor, Lecturer Percentage (Number)*	*Rank Difference*	*Total Percentage (Number)*
Humanities	3 (588)	7 (332)	12 (529)	30 (76)	27*	8 (1525)
Social Sciences	2 (490)	6 (298)	11 (441)	27 (90)	25*	8 (1319)
Biological Sciences	2 (393)	8 (235)	13 (287)	33 (42)	31*	8 (957)
Physical Sciences	1 (587)	3 (292)	5 (390)	4 (119)	3	3 (1388)
Total Academic Fields	2 (2058)	6 (1157)	10 (1647)	20 (327)	18*	7 (5189)

Source: Secondary Analysis of Carnegie Data.

*Statistically significant at the 0.05 level.

Table 10. Women Among Faculty with Doctorates by Rank and Number of Years at Institution

	Full Professor Percentage (Number)	*Associate Professor Percentage (Number)*	*Assistant Professor Percentage (Number)*	*Instructor, Lecturer Percentage (Number)*	*Rank Difference*	*Total Percentage (Number)*
Less than, or up to three years	2 (326)	5 (423)	7 (1513)	16 (291)	14*	7 (2553)
Four to six years	4 (296)	4 (533)	13 (633)	23 (71)	19*	8 (1533)
Seven or more years	2 (2391)	8 (833)	25 (142)	30 (76)	28*	5 (3442)
Total All Fields	2 (3013)	6 (1789)	10 (2288)	19 (438)	17*	6 (7528)

Source: Secondary Analysis of Carnegie Data.

*Statistically significant at the 0.05 level.

points. Among those who have been at the institution seven or more years, the rank difference in percentage of women is twenty-eight points. (See Table 10.)

The data demonstrate both the underutilization of those women who already belong to the pool of qualified persons in a national sample of faculty at high quality universities, and the differential distribution of women at the ranks of instructor and lecturer. Berkeley shows a similar pattern to the Carnegie data, but with only 5 percent women among the assistant professors, and 27 percent women among the instructors and lecturers (*Report of the Committee on Senate Policy,* page 25). At Berkeley, these latter ranks are separate, nonladder ranks, from which it is impossible to transfer into the ladder ranks assistant, associate, and full professor for promotion and tenure.

Colleges and universities are making tremendous progress in new appointments at the assistant professor level. As Robert Johnson pointed out in an earlier chapter, 27 percent of the new hires at Berkeley in 1973-1974 were women, compared to only 3 percent in 1967-1968, and similar progress has been reported by administrators at Stanford, Princeton, and Yale. In all four cases administrators have assured me that the caliber of new hires under affirmative action recruiting has increased, rather than decreased. This is an important refutation of the argument that affirmative action on behalf of women and minorities will destroy standards of scholarship and excellence. These kinds of results indicate that traditional recruitment patterns are changing. It is hoped that traditional patterns of promotion and tenure are also changing, and that the assistant professorship will not become a revolving door for women and minorities.

summary

This chapter has identified five major filtering points which have operated to keep women and minorities from achieving fullest potential in the educational system. Effective affirmative action for colleges and universities requires that special attention be given to these points:

1. Failure to take high school mathematics limits choice of undergraduate majors. Women and non-Asian minorities are systematically underrepresented in undergraduate majors requiring calcu-

lus. This requires improved counseling in high school to match changing role expectations for women and minorities.

2. Women and minorities are considerably less likely to plan to work for a doctorate. This requires raising levels of ambition and aspirations consistent with levels of talent and changing role expectations based on traditional sex and ethnic stereotypes.

3. Until very recently, women graduate students have had higher dropout rates than men. Attention needs to be paid to ways of increasing social support for women and minorities, to keep them in doctoral programs long enough to taste the rewards of success in the field.

4. Academic recruitment and hiring has been limited by reliance on the "old boy" or "buddy" system. Attention needs to be paid to opening up search and recruitment procedures to include qualified women and minorities, at ladder level appointments, rather than at dead end levels.

5. Promotion and tenure procedures need to be examined to make sure that standards of evaluation do not assume that, by definition, being female or a member of an ethnic minority are demerits.

references

Mooney, J. D. "Attrition among Ph.D. Candidates: An Analysis of Recent Woodrow Wilson Fellows." *Journal of Human Resources,* 1968, *3,* 47-62.

Report of the Committee on Senate Policy. Subcommittee on the Status of Academic Women on the Berkeley Campus, University of California. May 19, 1973.

Sells, L. W. *Preliminary Report on the Status of Graduate Women: University of California.* Berkeley, Calif., March 1973.

Trow, M., and others. *Technical Report: National Survey of Higher Education.* Carnegie Commission on Higher Education. Berkeley, Calif., 1972.

Lucy W. Sells is a political sociologist completing her doctoral dissertation at the University of California, Berkeley. She has served as a member of the Berkeley Chancellor's Advisory Committee on the Status of Women and of the Academic Senate Committees on the Status of Women and on Academic Planning, and she is the editor of two editions of the resource book, Current Research on Sex Roles.

Means of achieving effective affirmative action and resources which can be mobilized to this end.

new directions for affirmative action

lucy w. sells

This volume has provided a forum for examining the respective positions of the advocates, adversaries, and enforcers of affirmative action. Sandler, Hook, Todorovich, and Holmes gave positive, constructive examples of these three perspectives; and Johnson and Fleming point out the implications of affirmative action from the university administrator's perspective.

To summarize the points of disagreement leading to the current paralysis of affirmative action: (1) Advocates and enforcers both insist that goals are not quotas, while adversaries insist that goals are quotas by another name. (2) Advocates and enforcers both insist that lowering of standards are not required, while adversaries insist that lowering of standards is inevitable. (3) Advocates insist that the right to file suit in court is essential to preserve the rights of women and minorities, while adversaries insist that court suits are costly in time, energy, and money, and that binding arbitration, without recourse to court suits, is essential to preserve the integrity of institutions of higher education.

In terms of the first point, I believe the weight of the evidence, now that initial confusion has subsided, tends toward the advocates and enforcers. In terms of the second issue, everyone agrees that colleges and universities should not lower their standards. And even the adversaries, who reject the "industrial model" of affirmative action for the recruitment, hiring, and promotion of faculty because of the differences between universities and the construction firms for which Executive Order 11246 as amended was written, would probably agree that the industrial model should apply for university support staff: the vast army of typists, clerks, custodians, and other people who keep institutions of higher education functioning.

On the conflict between court suits to protect the rights of individuals versus binding arbitration to protect the autonomy of institutions, I propose a third alternative, which takes into account the needs both of individuals and of institutions. Court suits and binding arbitration both serve to polarize the perspectives of individuals and institutions, driving them further and further apart by setting up the situation of two hostile camps, dealing with each other as adversaries. The alternative to such a procedure is mediation, in which it is assumed that both parties share common values. Mediation frees both sides to develop constructive solutions to a mutual problem as advocates of both individuals and institutions.

the need for facts

Most immediately, however, achieving effective affirmative action requires facts about the differential distribution of women and minorities at all levels of power and authority within and outside of institutions of higher education in order to move everyone's fantasies about this distribution closer to reality. The best method is to encourage people to draw their own conclusions from the data, rather than trying to force conclusions on them. Discovered knowledge is more likely to be retained and made relevant to problems at hand than force fed knowledge. This approach is a synthesis of the best of Niccolo Machiavelli and Dale Carnegie. It gets results in converting adversaries to advocates of affirmative action.

The paralysis of the past four years on affirmative action is not part of some Machiavellian plot by the adversaries to keep women and minorities out of the reward structure of the educational system; nor is it a plot to destroy institutions of higher education by the advocates and enforcers; nor is it collusion to keep women and minorities out of the reward structure by the adversaries and enforcers. Rather, the paralysis results from the fact that people from all three perspectives are oblivious to their own unconscious, implicit assumptions about human behavior based on sex-role, ethnic-role, and authority-role stereotyping.

People at all levels of higher education have been open and receptive to data such as those in the preceding chapter, and they often comment on the causes and consequences of the data. A frequent response to the differential enrollments in high school mathematics is, "Is this really a problem? Maybe women don't take mathematics in high school because they don't *want* to. Shouldn't they have freedom of choice?" The question that needs to be asked is what happens differently to men and to women that makes men but not women want to continue with mathematics in high school. Contrary to the notion of some advocates and enforcers of affirmative action, most adversaries are reasonable people who are capable of seeing for themselves that freedom of choice depends on keeping options open as long as possible and that the mathematics filter closes options for women, and even more intensely for non-Asian minorities.

Longitudinal data on students such as those provided by the graduate division at Berkeley are a prime example of the importance of effective institutional research to dispel the myths held by advocates, adversaries, and enforcers of affirmative action. The reality is that attrition among women in graduate study at Berkeley is considerably lower in the 1970s than it was in the 1960s. In the long run, this institutionally initiated form of data gathering and analysis to assess progress on affirmative action will make a greater contribution to effective affirmative action than the kinds of data gathering and analysis currently imposed by the enforcers. At present, the enforcers view the extensive data gathering and analysis imposed on institutions as a necessary form of institutional consciousness raising which heightens the awareness of recruitment, hiring, and promotion practices that operate to filter out women and minorities.

National data such as that on Woodrow Wilson fellows can be particularly effective in demonstrating that affirmative action is necessary to achieve high standards of scholarship and excellence, so that the achievements of women and minorities rated *excellent* might surpass those of white men rated *average*. Armed with such knowledge, previous adversaries of affirmative action are free to contribute solutions to the problem.

The major targets for the educational process include:

- Students: Starting in junior high school, to raise their aspirations and motivations consistent with their ability levels, regardless of sex or ethnicity.
- Parents: To raise their expectations for their children, regardless of sex or ethnicity.
- Faculty, administrators, governing boards of institutions, state and federal legislators, and state and federal compliance enforcement agencies: To raise their expectations for students, and for each other, independently of sex, ethnicity, or level of authority.

resources for affirmative action

The most important resource for achieving effective affirmative action is the personal talents and energies of advocates of affirmative action working together to pull women and minorities into the availability pools. Speaking as one such advocate, we need to stop wasting our time and energies in fighting adversaries and enforcers over words on pieces of paper called affirmative action plans, and concentrate on producing the kinds of results in our respective fields that will qualify us for jobs and salaries consistent with abilities and ambitions. Decision makers at all levels of authority are more likely to accept our assistance in solving problems and our expressions of support, interest, and concern than they are to tolerate protest and outrage which implicitly accuse them of acting out of hostility and bad faith.

At the same time, institutions of higher education need to be free to run the risk of trusting enforcers that goals are not quotas and that as long as departments and institutions demonstrate good faith efforts in recruitment and search procedures they are under no compulsion to meet those goals. The crucial question from the advocates' perspective then becomes, "What constitutes good faith efforts, and who sets and defines the standards of 'qualified' persons?"

The second resource is the good will of persons at all levels who are already on the side of the advocates. People who suffer from discrimination or those who at any level of authority feel oppressed by those above and disappointed by those below are likely to be oblivious to the existence of good will on the part of others; but this good will does exist in a variety of forms and resources. A difficult political problem is to persuade people who have not yet tasted the rewards of success in their field that there are persons of good will who are on their side. Graduate students who are still agonizing over whether they want to make the commitment necessary for academic success need to recognize their supporters on the faculty. Faculty need to recognize theirs in the administration, just as administrations of institutions of higher education need to recognize theirs in Congress, and in the Department of Health, Education, and Welfare.

The third useful resource is the growing number of academic and professional organizations devoted to achieving effective affirmative action on behalf of women and minorities. Some of these are listed in the section on further information at the end of this article.

steps toward affirmative action

The first new direction for affirmative action is for advocates, adversaries, and enforcers of affirmative action to examine the data on discrimination and develop openness of communication among each other on that basis. The alternative direction has been to assume ill will and closed mindedness until there is direct evidence to counteract these. Experience has shown that this direction tends to become a self-fulfilling prophecy, and that most of us tend to live up to the expectations placed on us by others.

A second new direction is for advocates to accept for themselves a sense of autonomy, initiative, and responsibility, leading to results which will persuade evaluators and decision makers that they merit the same rewards others have succeeded in earning. Too many of us are spending all our energies trying to get acceptable affirmative action plans adopted in our respective institutions instead of producing the kind of intellectual and academic results that free us to compete on equal terms with white male colleagues. For those who have not yet gained success, this action may be perceived as selling out to the system. But this action merely uses the rules of the system to work for their success, rather than against it. Because of the heretofore closed nature of communication within educational institutions, part of the over-representation of white males at upper levels of educational systems probably stems from the fact that they have been more closely in touch with the rules for succeeding in those systems. Women and minorities can learn to play the same game.

A third new direction for effective affirmative action is to use the value of academic freedom in the context of the free marketplace of ideas to achieve a free marketplace of information about the rules for succeeding within the system at every level: adequate mathematics preparation to keep options open as an undergraduate; application to graduate school; survival in doctoral programs; and success in getting hired, promoted, and earning tenure at the highest levels consistent with abilities, energies, and aspirations, independently of sex or ethnicity. The ultimate solution to achieving effective affirmative action requires our freedom to elicit the best in ourselves and in others.

for further information

General information about federal laws and regulations is available in "Federal Laws and Regulations Concerning Sex Discrimination in Educational Institutions," produced by the Project on the Status and Education of Women of the Association of American Colleges. Copies are available from Information Office, Office for Civil Rights, U.S. Department of Health, Education, and Welfare, Washington, D.C. 20201.

Further information on specific federal laws and regulations may be obtained from the following sources:

Executive Order 11246, as amended by 11345.

Division of Higher Education
Office for Civil Rights
Department of HEW
Washington, D.C. 20201

or

Office of Federal Contract Compliance
Employment Standards Administration
Department of Labor
Washington, D.C. 20210

or

Regional HEW or DOL Office

Title VII of the Civil Rights Act of 1964, as amended by the Equal Employment Opportunity Act of 1972.

Equal Employment Opportunity Commission
1800 G Street, N.W.
Washington, D.C. 20506

or

Regional EEOC Office

Equal Pay Act of 1963, as amended by the Education Amendments of 1972 (Higher Education Act).

Wage and Hour Division
Employee Standards Administration
Department of Labor
Washington, D.C. 20210

or

Field, Area, or Regional Wage and Hour Office

Title IX of the Education Amendments Act of 1972 (Higher Education Act), and Title VII (Sections 799A and 845) of the Public Health Service Act, as amended by the Comprehensive Health Manpower Act of 1971.

Division of Higher Education
Office for Civil Rights
Department of HEW
Washington, D.C. 20201

or

Regional HEW Office

Women. The most comprehensive books on women in higher education now available are that edited by W. Todd Furniss and Patricia A. Graham stemming from the 1972 annual meeting of the American Council on Education, *Women in Higher Education* (Washington, D.C.: American Council on Education), and that edited by Alice S. Rossi and Ann M. Calderwood, *Academic Women on the Move* (New York: Russell Sage Foundation, 1973).

The Carnegie Commission on Higher Education addressed the question of women's rights in its September 1973 report, *Opportunities for Women in Higher Education: Their Current Participation, Prospects for the Future, and Recommendations for Action* (New York: McGraw-Hill, 1973). It also published *Antibias Regulation of Universities: Faculty Problems and Their Solutions,* by Richard A. Lester of Princeton University (McGraw-Hill, 1974)—a skillful analysis of the ways in which the enforcers have contributed to the paralysis of affirmative action, and a proposal for mediation and arbitration of discrimination claims through panels of mediator-arbitrators from comparable institutions rather than through court suits or adversary proceedings by external compliance agencies; *Escape From the Doll's House: Women in Graduate and Professional School Education,* by Saul D. Feldman (McGraw-Hill, 1974), an analysis of data from the commission's National Survey of Higher Education Faculty and Student Opinion; and a technical note, "Prospects for Minority-Group and Female Participation in Higher Education Faculties, 1970-2000," in the commission's final report, *Priorities for Action* (McGraw-Hill, 1973, pp. 107-127). The commission has scheduled a forthcoming book of essays on women in higher education, edited by Florence Howe.

A list of women's caucuses and committees in professional associations has been compiled by Ruth M. Oltman of the American Association of University Women. Copies can be obtained from the assistant director of Program—Higher Education, American Association of University Women, 2401 Virginia Avenue, N.W., Washington, D.C. 20037. In addition, the Federation of Organizations for Professional Women now exists at 1346 Connecticut Avenue, N.W., Washington, D.C. 20036, to coordinate the efforts of these associations.

Minorities. Black Educators in White Colleges, by William Moore, Jr., and Lonnie H. Wagstaff (San Francisco: Jossey-Bass, 1974) reports a study of 3228 black academics and devotes a special chapter (pp. 72-98) to affirmative action.

Among the literature on minority groups in higher education are survey reports on Black American Doctorates by James W. Bryant, available from the Office for Special Projects of the Ford Foundation, 320 East 43rd Street, New York, New York 10017, and on blacks in legal education and the law, available from the American Bar Association, 1155 60th Street, Chicago, Illinois 60637. Data on degrees attained by native Americans are available from the Bureau of Indian Affairs—Higher Education, 5301 Central Avenue, N.W., Albuquerque, New Mexico 87108. Data on Spanish-speaking doctorate holders can be obtained from the Cabinet Committee on Opportunity for the Spanish-Speaking, 1707 H Street, N.W., Washington, D.C. 20036.

The Carnegie Commission reviewed the problem of minority students in *A Chance to Learn: An Action Agenda for Equal Opportunities in Higher Education* (McGraw-Hill, 1970).

Advocates, Adversaries, and Enforcers. An impressive array of materials and information on affirmative action for women is available from The Project on the Status and Education of Women, directed by Bernice Sandler for the Association of American Colleges and available from project offices at 1818 R Street, N.W., Washington, D.C. 20009. Affirmative action for minorities is ably advocated by Bayard Rustin and Norman Hall, the executive director and associate director of the A. Philip Randolph Institute in "Affirmative Action in an Economy of Scarcity," available from the Institute at 260 Park Avenue South, New York, New York 10010. Illustrations of local documents from women's advocates include "Critique of the September 1974 Berkeley Affirmative Action Plan" by Isabel Pritchard, Charlene Harrington, and Andrea Sallychild ($1), and "Sex Discrimination in Physical Education and Athletics Programs in California Higher Education," by Marie Hart, Charlene Harrington, Susan Leal, and Cindy McGrath ($2), available from the Student Affirmative Action Committee, Academic Affairs Office, 204 Eshelman Hall, University of California, Berkeley, California 94720. Dorothy Legarreta's "The Berkeley Student Affirmative Action Plan" is available for $2 from the Third World and Women's Council, 516 Eshelman Hall, University of California, Berkeley, California 94720.

Among the adversaries of federal policies, John H. Bunzel, president of San Jose State University, has written "The Quota Mentality" for *Freedom at Issue,* November-December 1973, No. 22, pp. 10-14; and "The Politics of Quotas" for *Change,* October 1972, pp. 25, 30-35. Paul Seabury of the University of California wrote "HEW and the Universities" for *Commentary,* February 1972, pp. 38-44, and "The Idea of Merit" for *Commentary,* December 1972, pp. 41-45. Materials are also available from the Committee on Academic Nondiscrimination and Integrity, Second Floor, 444 Park Avenue South, New York, New York 10016, and from the University Centers for Rational Alternatives, 110 West 40th Street, New York, New York 10018.

From the enforcer's perspective, J. Stanley Pottinger's "The Drive Toward Equality," in *Change,* October 1972, pp. 24, 26-29, runs opposite Bunzel's article.

Turning to sociological analyses, Peter Blau's *The Organization of Academic Work* (New York: Wiley, 1973) neatly examines the inherent tension between faculty creativity and productivity on the one hand, which require flexibility and freedom to pursue one's ideas to the limit, and the rational constraints of administrators on the other hand to get things done efficiently and in a reasonable amount of time. His argument about the different needs of faculty and administrators highlights the difference between universities and industrial or business organizations. Finally, Jamie Beth Catlin, John A. Seeley, and Margaret Talburtt, doctoral students at the University of Michigan, have analyzed the impact of federal enforcement on that institution, and their conclusions appear in *Affirmative Action: Its Legal Mandate and Organizational Implications,* available for $3 from the Center for the Study of Higher Education, School of Education, University of Michigan, Ann Arbor, Michigan 48104.

index

Accountability, 7
Administrative Conference of the United States, 35
Advertising, affirmative, 7
Affirmative action: achievements in, 56-57; administrative problems in, 66-67; adversaries of, x-xi, 95-96; advocates of, ix-x, 95; conflict over, ix-xiii; costs of, 61-63; court decisions related to, 9, 10, 12-13, 17, 19; critical points for, 71-86; defined, 9, 40; diversity denied by, 68-69; enforcers of, xi, 96; facts needed for, 88-90; as federal interference, 15, 34, 45-47; further information on, 92-96; governmental implications of, 65-70; institutional implications of, 55-64; issues of, 4-8, 41-44; jurisdictional conflicts in, 67-68; legislation on, 1-21; myths and realities of, to an advocate, 8-19; myths and realities of, to an enforcer, 39-54; new directions for, 87-96; and numerical goals, 9-11; opportunities for, 57-61; publication of plans for, 8; resources for, 90-91; steps toward, 91-92; written plans for, 4
Affirmative Action Construction Program, 58-59
Alexander v. Gardner-Denver Co., 17
American Association of Presidents of Independent Colleges and Universities, 44, 45
American Association of University Women, 94
American Bar Association, 95
American Council on Education, 93
Andover Academy, 39
Anti-Defamation League, 26
Appellate boards, for cases of discrimination, 35-37
Arbitration: advantages of, 18, 67-68; dangers of, 16-19, 87-88, 94
Arkansas, 49
Association of American Colleges, Project on the Education and Status of Women, 4, 21, 48, 92, 95
Authoritarianism, concept of, xii
Availability pools, defined, 82

Blau, P., 96
Bryant, J. W., 94
Bunzel, J. H., 50, 52, 95, 96
Bureau of Indian Affairs, 95

Cabinet Committee on Opportunity for the Spanish-Speaking, 95
Calderwood, A. M., 94
California, 61
California, University of: at Berkeley, xiii, 35, 40, 42, 55-64, 72-77, 80-81, 85, 89, 95; at Davis, 57; at Los Angeles, 57; at San Diego, 56; at San Francisco, 56; at Santa Cruz, 56
Carnegie Commission on Higher Education, 71*n*, 81-82, 83*n*, 85, 94, 95
Catlin, J. B., 96
Child care, 6
Civil Rights Acts of 1866 and 1871, 4, 19
Civil Rights Act of 1964, 23, 40; Title VII of, 1, 3, 4, 5, 6, 7, 10, 11, 15, 17, 18, 19, 24, 59, 93
Committee on Academic Nondiscrimination and Integrity, 23, 24, 29, 38, 96
Commonwealth of Philadelphia v. O'Neill, 12-13
Cypress v. Newport News General and Non-Sectarian Hospital Association, 10

Data collection: benefits of, 20; costs of, 62
Department of Health, Education, and Welfare, xii, 2, 3, 5, 6, 7, 8, 10, 14, 15, 19, 20, 25, 26, 27, 28, 31, 33, 34, 37, 40, 42, 45, 46, 47, 48,

49, 50, 51, 52, 53, 54, 61, 67; Office of Civil Rights of, xi, 23-24, 39, 40, 41, 44, 45, 46, 47, 48-49, 50, 51, 52, 92, 93
Department of Labor, 20, 31, 33, 45, 46, 48, 67; Employment Standards Administration, 2-3, 93; Office of Federal Contract Compliance, 2, 23, 46, 92
Dewey, J., 23
Directives on nondiscrimination, 33-34
Due process, lack of, 66-67

Educational Opportunity Program (EOP), 56-57, 60
Education Amendments Act of 1972, Title IX of, 2, 3, 4, 19, 21, 59, 93
Education and Labor, Committee on, Special Subcommittee on Education, xi-xii, 21, 27, 29
EEOC v. University of New Mexico, 19
Employment, conditions of, 7
Enforcement, impact of, 48-49
Equal Employment Opportunity Commission (EEOC), 3, 10, 17, 18, 20, 31, 36, 37, 67, 93
Equal Pay Act of 1963, 1-3, 5, 18-19, 93
Equity, concept of, 9
Executive Order 11246, 1, 2, 4, 5, 6, 7, 8, 9, 10, 11, 19, 21, 23, 31, 33, 40, 41, 45-46, 51, 52, 63, 88, 92-93

Federation of Organizations for Professional Women, 94
Feldman, S. D., 94
Fleming, R. W., xiii, 65-70, 87
Ford Foundation, 94
Freedom of Information Act, 19
Furniss, W. T., 93

Goals: court ordered and executive ordered, 12; defined, 9; numerical, 2, 4, 8, 9-11; as quotas, 25-27, 50-51, 87; and timetables, 4-5, 24, 32-33, 41, 53
Graduate school, as critical point: application to, 76-78, 86; support during, 78-81, 86, 89
Graham, P. A., 93
Green, A. A., 13, 21
Grievance procedures, 6, 35-37
Griggs v. Duke Power Co., 17

Hall, N., 95
Harrington, C., 95
Hart, M., 95
HEW. *See* Department of Health, Education, and Welfare
Hiring: criteria for, 12, 16; inbred, 7
Holmes, P. E., xi, 27, 39-54, 65, 87
Hook, S., x, 23-29, 48, 51, 52, 87
Howe, F., 94

International Association of Official Human Rights Agencies, 10

Job analysis, 8
Job classification, defined, 53
Johnson, R. L., xiii, 55-64, 85, 87

Leal, S., 95
Lea v. Cone Mills, 10
Legarreta, D., 95
Legislation, 1-21, 92-93
Lester, R. A., 13, 15, 21, 94
Louisiana, 49
Louisiana v. United States, 9

McGrath, C., 95
Marital and parental status, 7
Marquez v. Ford Motor Co., 12
Maternity leave, 6, 20, 57
Mathematics, high school, as critical point, 71-75, 85-86, 89
Mediation, 88, 94
Michigan, University of, xiii, 13, 21, 68, 96
Minnesota, University of, 14
Minorities, further information on, 94-95
Minority Vendor Program, 58
Mitchell, J., 79*n*
Monitoring, 7, 63
Mooney, J. D., 78, 79*n*, 86
Moore, W., Jr., 94
Moynihan, D. P., 39

Nepotism, 6, 57
Neusner, J., 28
New Mexico, 49
New York, State University of, 33-34

New York University, 36, 37
Nixon, R. M., 5, 27
Nondiscrimination, suggestions for, 33-38
Numerical goals. *See* Goals

Oklahoma, 49
Oltman, R. M., 94

Part-time status, 8
Pensions, 5-6, 20
Policy statements, on nondiscrimination, 7
Pottinger, J. S., 96
Powell, W., 17-18
Preferential treatment: and HEW, 26, 49-53; myths and realities of, 11-16
Princeton University, 85
Pritchard, I., 95
Promotions: affirmative action in, 44-45; as critical point, 82-85, 86

Randolph Institute, A. Phillip, 95
Recruitment: affirmative action in, 42-43; costs of, 61-62; as critical point, 81-82, 86; diversity in, 68-69; nondiscriminatory practices in, 6; "old boy" method of, 15, 81-82, 86; preferential treatment in, 11-12
Retirement, 5-6, 20, 57
Reverse discrimination, myth of, 13-14
Revised Order No. 4, 44-45
Rossi, A. S., 94
Rustin, B., 95

Salary, 5
Sallychild, A., 95
Sanctions, graded, 35
Sandler, B., x, 1-21, 48, 65, 87, 95
Seabury, P., 40, 42, 44, 95
Search committees, 7
Seeley, J. A., 96
Sells, L. W., ix-xiii, 71-96
Stanford University, 85
State of Alabama v. United States, 10
Statistics, abuse of, 32-33
Students, affirmative action programs for, 8, 56-57, 59-61

Talburtt, M., 96
Termination rates, 8
Texas, 49
TIAA, 5-6
Time limit, for bureaucratic decisions, 34-35, 46-47
Title VII. *See* Civil Rights Act of 1964
Title IX. *See* Education Amendments Act of 1972
Todorovich, M. M., x, 31-38, 87
Training: employee, 57-58; in-service, 8
Trow, M., 81, 85

Underutilization, defined, 53
University Centers for Rational Alternatives, 26, 29, 38, 96
Utilization, defined, 82

Vetter, J., 35

Wagstaff, L. H., 94
Women: further information on, 93-94; minority, 8
Women's Equity Action League (WEAL), 21, 83*n*
Woodrow Wilson Fellows, 78-80, 81, 89
Work assignments, 8

Yale University, 85

NEW DIRECTIONS QUARTERLY SOURCEBOOKS

New Directions for Institutional Research is one of three quarterly publications of Jossey-Bass Inc., Publishers. Each series provides concise, practical, and timely assistance on a pressing educational topic. Topics and issue editors for each series are listed below.

Yearly subscription rates for each series are $25 for institutions, libraries, and agencies, and $15 for individuals when paid by personal check. To subscribe, or to receive further information, write: *New Directions* Subscriptions, Jossey-Bass Inc., Publishers, 615 Montgomery Street, San Francisco, California 94111.

NEW DIRECTIONS FOR HIGHER EDUCATION
JB Lon Hefferlin, Editor-in-Chief

1973–1. *Facilitating Faculty Development,* Mervin Freedman
2. *Strategies for Budgeting,* George Kaludis
3. *Services for Students,* Joseph Katz
4. *Evaluating Learning and Teaching,* Robert Pace

1974–5. *Encountering the Unionized University,* Jack Schuster
6. *Implementing Field Experience Education,* John Duley
7. *Avoiding Conflict in Faculty Personnel Practices,* Richard Peairs
8. *Improving Statewide Planning,* James Wattenbarger, Louis Bender

NEW DIRECTIONS FOR COMMUNITY COLLEGES
Arthur M. Cohen, Editor-in-Chief
Florence B. Brawer, Associate Editor

1973–1. *Toward a Professional Faculty,* Arthur Cohen
2. *Meeting the Financial Crisis,* John Lombardi
3. *Understanding Diverse Students,* Dorothy Knoell
4. *Updating Occupational Education,* Norman Harris

1974–5. *Implementing Innovative Instruction,* Roger Garrison
6. *Coordinating State Systems,* Edmund Gleazer, Roger Yarrington
7. *From Class to Mass Learning,* William Birenbaum
8. *Humanizing Student Services,* Clyde Blocker

NEW DIRECTIONS FOR INSTITUTIONAL RESEARCH
Sidney Suslow, Editor-in-Chief
Paul Jedamus, Associate Editor

1974–1. *Evaluating Institutions for Accountability,* Howard Bowen
2. *Assessing Faculty Effort,* James Doi
3. *Toward Affirmative Action,* Lucy Sells